Jacquelyn
Smithson
Howard

From

Out

Of

The

Shadows

Sandra O. Smithson

Doubt in the
Service of
Faith
& Other
Paradoxes

From Out of The Shadows – Doubt in The Service of Faith and Other Paradoxes

Copyright 2020 by Sandra O. Smithson and Jacquelyn Smithson Howard

Cover Design and Art Work by Graffiti Bleu Worldwide (info@gbleu.com)

Chapter graphics from motionarray.com and pixabay.com

This book is a series of reflections by the authors to address the paradox of asking questions. The very word "quest/i/on" attempts to ask, "What-quest-am-I-on?" All of the reflections within seek to answer that question.

Published in the United States of America
Sunshine Solutions Publishing
9912 Business Park Drive #170
Sacramento, CA 95827

Library of Congress: 2020919948
ISBN: 9798695729122

Contents

FOREWORD

The real challenge of human life is one of faith in the Divine Source of all life. But the paradox of faith is that it is at once both darkness and light. And the mystery of this paradox is that the brighter the light, the deeper the darkness; and the deeper the darkness the brighter the light.

Christ asked this question of His Apostles: "Think you that the Son of Man will find faith on the earth when He comes again?"

It was not an idle question, for the more we are able to glean of tried and proven knowledge through the advances of science and technology, the further away we are drawn from the "habit" of faith. And the more we become wedded to our own inventions and conclusions, the further away we are drawn from the practice of internal reflection and the joy of interpersonal relationships. The end result is that we become alienated from God, each other, and even our very own *self*. God is *Person*, and there can be no interaction with God except that which is personal. Likewise, we cannot know each other nor our own self, for it is the divine Image that ultimately defines us. But we cannot be defined according to the Image which enhances our truest self, without contemplation. *"The Kingdom of God,"* Christ taught us, *"is within you."*

This book has no real chapters, those conventional lines of demarcation, for life is like that - no clear beginnings, no clear endings.

This book, then, is a meditative collage, a few sparks from the shafts of light that momentarily shattered my interior darkness during those quiet moments when I was "faithful" enough and "free" enough to rest in the shadows.

Sandra O. Smithson, O.S.F.

It happened that one of the Twelve,
Thomas (the name means "Twin"),
was absent when Jesus came. The
other disciples kept telling him: "We
have seen the Lord!" His answer was,
"I will never believe it without probing
the nail prints in His hands, without
putting my finger in the nail marks
and my hand into His side."

John 20: 24-25

1   Cracking Open

The apostle, Thomas, isn't often singled out by Holy Mother Church to receive much attention, and certainly nothing of praise. He was the *doubter*, the one who couldn't get the message for the media; the one who, to the shame of all the faithful who would be forever "blest" for not demanding proof, held out against the mounting wave of emotion that followed the hearsay testimony of the other women and men, apostles all, who claimed to have "seen the risen Lord."

Thomas is not your usual apostle for accolades. There have been no great books written to honor him, no great sermons preached to his memory. He, himself, wrote no canonically approved Gospels, those miniature biographies of the Lord that, for so many, contain the final solution to every problem. He didn't send out any grand epistles setting down for the edification and, sometimes, confusion, and certainly a continual debating game for all generations, his own doctrinal and dogmatic interpretation of the Savior's mind. He made no effort to "scientize" the Savior's lofty ideal of trust and love by reducing it to a system of theology. All he did for the good of posterity was simply *to doubt* the testimony. John does not say that Thomas doubted Jesus, nor God - simply the testimony. He doubted the testimony!

And yet for this detestable behavior, a scandal to everybody except, perhaps, Jesus Himself who knew and understood the frailty of human nature, he was rewarded by the Lord in a special way that not too many since would be able to boast. He was allowed *to touch* Jesus. And this "touching" of Jesus brought about the most believable, the most indisputable and incontestable testimony for all the rest that the Lord had, indeed, risen from the dead. "Put your finger in the wounds of my hand and your hand into my side, and be not faithless but believing." And Thomas, having probed those terrible gouges, was able to profess his faith with deep love and profound conviction: "My Lord and my God!"

At no previous time and by no other apostle before that incident, had there been such a clear and unmistakable profession of faith in the fullness of the nature of Jesus, one so unequivocal that even theologians would not be able to confuse its meaning.

Certainly Martha had gotten close when her urgency on behalf of her dead brother, Lazarus, had prompted her to remind Jesus of her understanding of His power and mission: "Lord, if you had been here, my brother would never have died...I have come to believe that you are the Messiah, the Son of God who is to come into the world." And Peter had edged in also when he responded to the Lord's question, "Who do you say that I am?" with much the same insight as Martha. Peter responded, "Thou art the Christ, the Son of the Living God."

Yes, Martha and Peter and even the Samaritan women had arrived at the belief that there was a special relationship between Jesus and God. They recognized Jesus as God's ambassador, the One called and anointed, the One commissioned by Yahweh, singled

9

out and raised up in their midst to save them, though they didn't know yet from what. But it was through the doubting Thomas, and the Lord's rewarding of his demand for proof, that we have the first full revelation about Jesus: He is God, Himself, God, incarnated.

If we have, with characteristic self-righteousness, thumbed our sanctimonious noses at what we consider a failing in Thomas, Jesus certainly did not, for Jesus was much more realistic about human frailty. We have focused on the state of "blessedness" of those who need no proof, as witnessed by the *words* of Jesus, and we have ignored the invitation to intimacy given to those who seek proof, as witnessed by the *example* of Jesus. "Come, Thomas, put your hand in My side."

Thomas is the apostle for our age, the apostle of the post-resurrection, for surely when, as Peter tells us, "The devil is roaming like a roaring lion," and Paul warns, "There will come teachers having itching ears," it behooves us to constantly test the spirit, to examine and reexamine all assumptions. Perhaps, in Thomas, Christ was teaching us the dramatic lesson of the "efficacy" of doubt. Doubt is not just the shady midground between belief and unbelief. Doubt is its own unique being with the potential of becoming a powerful catalyst. Total disbelief disengages us, robs us of motivation and meaning; and total belief runs the risk of lulling us to passivity, of leaving us sometimes to rely on deliverance despite our disengagement. But *doubt* has the power, if somewhat sinister, dubious, even sneaky, of constantly plaguing us, keeping us involved, of holding us to the search, of destroying our complacency, of rendering our position so uncomfortable that it challenges us to risk. We need to know, and so we keep reaching out. And, finally, in this constant reaching out, sooner or later we do touch Jesus.

In spite of Jesus' reaction to Thomas' doubt, the reward He offered him and the beautiful life-embracing testimony that flowed from him, we have clung to our suspicions about the wholesomeness of doubt and have so maligned it that we have actually constructed a system to render it not merely ineffectual, but downright inadmissible. Witness, for example, the doctrine of infallibility. When the leader of Roman Catholics speaks from his position as Head of the Church, our dogma maintains that he can't make a mistake. And to further prove our point against doubt, we cite the famous plight of the doubting Moses who was denied the promised land, and of the doubting Zachary who lost the power of speech. And then we go on to probe the teachings of the Lord on the power and rewards of real faith. We emphasize that Christ taught us that, if we believe, we can cure and be cured. And that's no small power in a creation destined for death and decay, in a world of constantly changing matter. If we believe, and our faith need only be the size of a mustard seed, we can uproot the mighty oaks and have them fall into the sea. Poison and the scorpion's bite will leave us unharmed. Jesus offered all these guarantees to the believer. Martha and Mary were given back their brother. Peter walked on water and was commissioned to "feed" the flock. The blind were freed to the brightness of light, and the lame danced in the streets. Thus, Christ praised and rewarded *faith* with healings and resurrections. But

11

it was in His own moment of doubt that He was able to give us the greatest healing, the greatest resurrection, the most precious and most enduring of all gifts: the gift of eternal life.

How did *DOUBT* bring about this cataleptic spiritual change for our depraved, deprived, and fallen humanity? The tinge of doubt that would test the faith of Christ had already been foreshadowed in His words, "And I, *if* I be lifted up from the earth, will draw all things to Myself." He knew His mission. He knew to what He had been called: "I have a baptism with which I am to be baptized, and how I am to be straightened until it be accomplished!" But He was not given the certainty of the outcome. "*If* I be lifted up…" And the doubt that pervaded His faith, that rendered His position torturous, "He sweat blood," and called Him to this risk, reached its zenith in the pathetic cry from the cross, "My God, My God, why hast Thou abandoned Me!"

His doubt had gripped Him fully, but it did not destroy Him. On the contrary, it propelled Him to the very bosom of the Father, to the risk of full and unqualified surrender: "Into Your hands, O Lord, I commend my Spirit."

No one seems to have given much attention to Christ's doubt. In fact, we have regarded this condition of doubt as so odious that we actually think ourselves blasphemous if we associate it with Christ. We talk about His love, His tenderness, His need for friends, His fear, His anger, even the fact that He was tempted. But we don't touch His doubt, and yet it is an inevitable part of the human condition, and Christ was fully human. Indeed, if we dared to, we might have to concede that, had there been no doubt in Him, it is doubtful that there could have been any temptation. And we know that Christ was tempted, and it was an ordeal that left Him so broken that He was in need of assistance, The Gospel says simply: "Angels came and ministered to Him."

Even the Gospel writers, it seems, could not deal with Christ's expression of doubt. They tried to explain away His "*If* I be lifted up..." by calling it a prophesy of His crucifixion. But "death on the cross" could hardly be predicated as a means of "drawing all men" to Himself. Death is the common lot of all creation and has never been universally thought of as attractive. And crucifixion was the fate of quite a few under the power of Rome. No one, thus condemned, had gained a following as a consequence of such condemnation. It was not on the death, but on the resurrection that salvation depended, as St. Paul testifies: "If Christ be not risen, our faith is in vain, and we are, of all peoples, the most to be pitied." So, it was precisely relative to His resurrection that Christ had to grapple with the human experience of doubt. "*If* I be lifted up from the earth..." That is - *If* I rise from the tomb. This God-Man, who could rightly claim: "The Father and I are one...Phillip, he who sees Me sees the Father,"...this Man was to drink the cup of doubt to the dregs and experience the deepest pain that flowed from it, giving full testimony of His truly human nature: "My God, My God why hast Thou abandoned Me?" And yet, despite this moment of doubt, impinging upon a life of Faith - real Faith - as His life had demonstrated, He could still quietly commend His Spirit to the Lord, and God rewarded Him by raising Him up. No wonder, then, after His own excruciating experience of doubt and the Father's gift of resurrection, thus His response to Thomas took the form of such tender intimacy, showed such depth of sympathetic understanding.

If faith brings the power of healing and doubt the invitation to intimacy, it is, perhaps, that these two are not really opposed to each other, but rather the upper and undersides of the same piece of cloth. Both are admissions of uncertainty, of darkness. Both attest to personal insufficiency and limitation, to a dependency on something other than one's own natural power. The difference is not really qualitative, but temperamental. They both express inadequacy and need, and so draw forth the saving action of a merciful God.

The opposite pole of faith, then, is not *doubt* but *certainty*. If *faith* and *doubt* have given such life to the people of God, *certainty* has almost been the death knoll. It has almost been the undoing of the Church. *Certainty* has put the warrior on his horse when the Lord asked for peace. Notwithstanding the Lord's admonition to Peter, "Put your sword back into its sheath. Those who use the sword are sooner or later destroyed by it...," we have the old theological arguments well entrenched in us for the justification of "capital punishment, so-called justifiable homicide, and even dare to refer to some wars as holy." We can't forget the Council of Clermont in 1095 and Pope Urban II's stirring sermon in which he sought to have the Christians stop killing each other by unifying them to

14

kill somebody else. The cause was, ostensibly, to "save the holy places from the infidel Turks," but Jesus had already rendered that excuse untenable. "My kingdom is not of this world..." Even the children got in on the act before it was finally over. Closer to the lived experience of Jesus is the posture of Mahatma Gandhi: "I know many causes for which I am prepared to die, but not one for which I am prepared to kill."

But that last point is a digression. The point is that *Certainty* "put the warrior on his horse," when the Lord asked for peace. And *Certainty* has given birth to animosity and suspicion, when the Lord asked for love and understanding. And *Certainty* has constructed the walls of schism and separation, when the Lord prayed for unity. *Certainty* has hallowed traditions even when these no longer serve any purpose but stagnation, and it has contributed to the entrenchment of laws even when these have proven to be oppressive. *Certainty* has enshrined itself in the judgment seat, when the Lord clearly warns, "Judge not." It has obstructed inquiry and mounted inquisitions. It has "anathematized" books that later proved to be prophetic; burned "heretics" who later were canonized; and canonized legends who later were debunked as mythological.

Yes, *Certainty* might very well be the most devastating disease to afflict the human race, one so intractable and detestable that even the healing hand of the Lord will not touch it. "Because you say, 'I see'," Christ warned the Pharisees, "you shall die in your sin."

"Breaking Open"

Two of them [Disciples] that same day were making their way to a village named Emmaus, seven miles distant from Jerusalem, discussing as they went, all that had happened. In the course of their lively exchange, Jesus approached and began to walk with them. However, they were restrained from recognizing Him. He said to them: "What are you discussing as you go your way." They halted in distress, and one of them, Cleopas by name, asked Him, "Are you the only resident of Jerusalem who does not know the things that went on there these past few days?" He said to them, "What things?" They said, "All those that had to do with Jesus of Nazareth, a prophet powerful in word and deed in the eyes of God and all the people; how our chief

16

priests and leaders delivered Him up to be condemned to death and crucified Him. We were hoping that He was the one who would set Israel free. Besides all this, today, the third day since these things happened, some women in our group have first brought us some astonishing news. They were at the tomb before dawn and failed to find the body, but returned with the tale that they had seen a vision of Angels who declared that He was alive."

Tagore writes: "I thought that my voyage had come to an end at the last limit of my power, that the path before me was closed, that provisions were exhausted and the time come to take shelter in silent obscurity. But I find that Thy will knows no end in me. And when old words die out on my tongue, new melodies break forth from the heart; and where the old tracks are lost, new country is revealed with its wonders."

2   Blessings

I hadn't given up. Giving up was not a part of my family history. But I needed to be recharged. As I sank into subconscious reflection, the images began to unfold. Images from the shadows that I refused to open up to the Light. I saw myself sitting quietly in the sun porch, the late afternoon solar rays stroking me with their thermal touch. The house was empty and soundless except for an occasional gurgle from the plugged-in coffee pot. My mind drifted to a painting by Helena Steffensmeier, a Franciscan nun, which hung on the living room wall. There, Jesus sat tall above the two Emmaus disciples, a cup of wine in His hand. Jesus was the Stranger who became the Host, the Guest who bought the blessing. The remembrance should have made me happy. Instead, I slipped into a deep sadness, was sucked down into it like an unwary organism caught in quicksand. I let it take me deep into its entrails, into its dark, empty cavern. And because I didn't struggle, it gentled itself, became quiet, and showed me its many faces.

In that hazy moment of reflection, the Christ was there, headless, heartless, handless - an empty shell. Defenseless, waiting, a broken discarded manikin, condemned, waiting for the descending weight of our unrepentance that would crush out the last of His life. I did not move. I did not attempt to understand nor analyze. The thought was filled with too much pain - like that of my childhood as I was growing up Black in the segregated South and my Church made no place for me in its school – even many of its pews. But now, here

19

was the Savior, offering Himself for destruction. Then He moved, and it was no longer He, but myself. Then it was both of us together. We were one thing, waiting to be crushed.

"I have come that all may have life."

The echo bounced off the inner walls of the deep well of my consciousness and dug into my resisting flesh like an electric drill chewing through hardened rock. A burst of blinding light filled the hollow. The exquisite pain quickened me. It was only a second. I opened my eyes. The earth was a blue, grey shadow. The dying sun farewelled the sky with flamboyant imprints heralding its passing. I watched it gradually fade away and leave its mission to the moon. I was not startled, but pondered, "Where was my imagination taking me?" I tried to focus, but it wasn't finished.

The coffee pot gurgled. Jesus sat tall above the two disciples of Emmaus, a cup of blessing in His hand. I saw myself go into the kitchen and get a bottle of wine and a small wheat bun that a friend had baked and handed to me. What friend? I didn't know. I did not move, but somehow, from the china cabinet in the dining room, I took the wooden chalice and plate. I didn't remember where it had come from, but it was clearly a reminder of my years of service as a "missionary" from the North American Church to the Latin American Church. My mind drifted back to the sun parlor, now dimmed by the evening shadows, I lit a candle. The Bread was there, and the Wine, and the Cup. I needed only a friend. Someone who believed in Him.

20

Someone who longed for Him as I did. Someone who was constantly in search of Him as I was. And then we would break the Bread, as He had instructed us who believe, in memory of Him. I knew we would find Him again in some new, unexpected way, in the breaking of the Bread.

"Christ Blessing the Child"

Then, He said to them, "What little sense you have! How slow you are to believe all the prophets have announced! Did not the Messiah have to undergo all this so as to enter into His glory? Beginning, then, with Moses and all the prophets, He interpreted for them every passage of Scripture which referred to Him....

3   Listen

If *certainty* isolates us behind a wall of intolerance and incommunicability, I'd like to suggest that *doubt* has the effect on the mind that a farmer's plow has on a waiting field. The plow overcomes resistance and opens the soil to receive new seed. *Doubt*, then, has all the possibilities of generating new life, contrary to popular belief. Suppose, instead of thinking we possessed all truth, we decided, instead, that our positions are tenuous, our propositions shaky, our search only begun. Suppose we approached all being and experience as the repository of a new insight, waiting to be gleaned, a new mystery to be probed, one that holds within itself another thread of the one fabric of truth - not conclusive, not final, not absolute, but contributive.

If I labor over this question of *Doubt*, if I seek to remove the stigma from it and give it an honorable place, it is because all of us have been the victims of *Certainty's* parade of miscalculations. We are all aware of these miscalculations, from the circumcising of the Gentiles in the infant church on to and beyond the shelving of Chardin in our own sophisticated times.

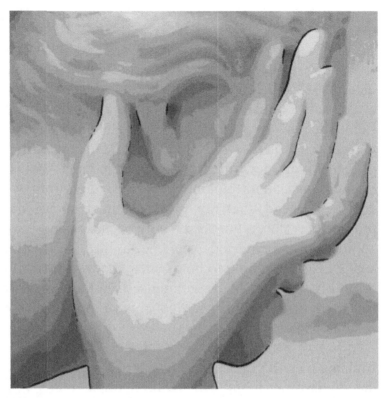

"The Listener"

We've choked at the gagging of Galileo, and we've sizzled at the burning of Joan of Arc. But we've done it so quietly. Never with the boldness of the Baptist at the Jordan's edge, nor the zeal of the converted Saul in the Council of Jerusalem. We have only whispered behind closed doors, unaware that the failure of *Certainty* may very well be the prod by which the Lord pricks us to the remembrance of our fallibility, of our need for constant doubt, watchfulness, and continual search. Perhaps, it is His merciful way of saving us from self-sufficiency and the fallacious, nefarious sense of absolute power that flows from it, rendering it impossible for us to become a credible sign of His presence in the world. A sign always stands for something other than itself, and its efficacy is in proportion to the degree and clarity by which it expresses and directs toward that for which it stands. So, John the Baptist, the Precursor, who made himself a living desert sign pointing toward the Christ, is also a sign for us of both the meaning and the means of our religious institutions, and leaders, however holy, however pretentious: "I must decrease; He must increase." Self -sufficiency has the opposite effect. If our institutions and our leaders could throw off the yoke of Self-sufficiency, and the virtue of *doubt* is an efficacious aid, then they could become the Sacrament of Hope to a straining world, forever in process; and through an honest, open search, bring the reaching, probing fingers of humankind closer to touching the mystery of Christ and the healing, creative Spirit that flows from Him. The other way, it seems, stops the unfolding of life, attempts to bind the free flow of this same Spirit, and mummify it by encasing it in suppressive laws and questionable dogmas, and burying it beneath sterile traditions.

But if our religious institutions and our religious leaders have any significance, any right to exist, isn't it in order to satisfy the longing of the human heart, summed up in the request of the Greeks to the apostle, Phillip, "Sir, we want to see Jesus." That is why we must continually *doubt* the testimony so that we will be moved always to examine and re-examine every face put before us by these institutions and leaders to see if these faces are, in fact, true reflections of this Jesus whom we seek. And we will know, finally - really know - as we grow in prayer and contemplation. "Be still and see that I am God." His promise is, "They shall all be taught of God." Be still and see that, "The Kingdom of God is within you." Therefore, no assumption should be held as too ancient or too sacred for this scrutiny. A false proposition does not cease to be false simply because it is tenacious, contributes to someone's personal comfort, buttresses private prejudices, or grows daily in popularity.

Perhaps, the truest, most sanctifying words spoken by the Roman Pontiff were spoken when he was asked about homosexuality: He stated, "Who am I to judge." He could have given the facile answer flowing through many Christian and other theologies, but the facile answer is, for the very fact of being facile, deserving of suspicion.

Our call is to Truth, and Truth is a larger terrain than mere answers. An answer is but a tiny glimmer of light and, at best, it only serves to make us more aware of the larger expanse of surrounding darkness that lies between us and the fullness of Light, this Jesus whom we seek. Is this cause for despair? I think it need not be. We will always be approaching that Son, God incarnate, from a dark spot in the shadows, always reaching toward the illimitable mystery of God from the disadvantaged position of infinitesimal limitation.

We approach God through a veil. Our intellect must deal with images and symbols. And the very symbols that we use to make possible a rational contemplation of His Being, because of their created and sensory nature, actually serve more to obscure than to unveil His Reality. As soon as we define, we limit, and therefore distort. If we are to know Him at all, it will be an intuitive experience of Him in that deep center, that dark inner well of our being that is so beyond the reach of human power that both the initiative and the fruition are entirely His action. "Peter, flesh and blood did not reveal this to you, but My Father who is in heaven." Is that not perhaps why He did not invite us to search for Him in dogmas and definitions? Instead He taught, "The kingdom of God is within you." and "Be still and know that I am God."

This is essentially the problem with theology, it seems. It is a rational approach to God. It is a logical construct. And the attempt to reduce God to a science, to capture Him in a rational system, or limit His Spirit and movement to the caprices of human authority and institutions, even to Sacraments in which the purpose is reduced by our "*ex opere operato*" theology can only lead to deception, confusion, and division - all symbolized in the story of the "Tower of Babel."

None of what I have said so far is meant to be an invitation to personal license nor public anarchy. Quite the contrary, law and order, rightly understood, are essential elements of freedom, growth, and creativity. The problem occurs, it seems to me, when law, itself, ceases to follow the same dynamic of growth and development that its right exercise makes possible outside of itself. When this happens, law and order lose their value as a freeing force generating life and creativity, and become, instead, suppressive, even deadly, because they tend, then, to exist for their own sake, to become ends rather than means. If there are any immutable laws, and I suspect there are none, it may be those inherent in the very nature of a being by which that being defines itself so as to be distinguished from another, and, according to which it develops or degenerates organically or in relationship. Outside of these intrinsic laws, we are dealing not only with the possibility but with the absolute necessity of mutability since all temporal life, individually in isolation, or collectively in society, is in a state of constant change, discovery, and alteration. No materiality nor temporality will ever have the power to lead us to the ultimate of Divine Truth, which is pure Spirit.

This is why all dogma is suspect, and every human answer is but an invitation to a new question. And this is so, because all reality is involved in mystery of which God is the ultimate, the all-pervasive, and the most elusive. He transcends all human categories and symbols.

We human beings must learn to be comfortable with God as mystery, must doubt each present position as final, as complete, and must remain open to constant readjustment, growth and change as we evolve toward Him. The last word, leading us to God, will never be spoken in this life - certainly not by us. But when it is spoken, it will be by the God who reigns on the throne of the Kingdom that He has established within us. To that conclusion, and only that, we will be held accountable. "If your conscience does not accuse you, you have not sinned."

"The Father, Son, and Holy Spirit"

What, then, does it mean to call oneself a "Person of Faith?" Scripture declares: "A just man lives by FAITH." What does real participation in the Ecclesial Community require of us?

4   Love

They will know we are Christians by our love... The new commandment called for Christians to be identified by this virtue. I took a deep breath as I thought of it. Love - what a wonderful reflection one could make as, each year, we look forward to the emotional end of winter ice and snow and lean into the promise of spring. Love! Can one doubt the power of love? The line from a popular song jumped to the front of my consciousness. "Hello young lovers wherever you are," I stopped it. Didn't want to go there. No, I needed to go deeper, to take the subject beyond the chemical attraction of young lovers that locks them into exclusivity.

Love takes many forms, but the love that truly matters, that encapsulates the transforming power secured in the redemptive action of Christ, is exactly the OPPOSITE of all that the word "exclusivity" implies. And yet, the exclusivity created by the chemical attraction of two lovers is an early realization of what love is really all about. It is a sort of primary school in this virtue that we call love. It is natural and has elements of regeneration because it seeks the good of the Loved One; it seeks to bring joy and pleasure to the Loved One; it establishes a unity of two by seeking to settle differences quickly and avoid conflicts. It searches for compromise; it seeks to shield the Loved One from pain; it protects the Loved One's reputation; it enhances the Loved One's social reputation and attends and contributes to the Loved One's physical and spiritual well-being.

This primary state of love through chemical attraction is built into our DNA and is unavoidable. It is God's first lesson to us that we are not created to be alone, as the story of Adam and Eve reveals; not created to be self-sufficient, but rather to need one another in order to fulfill one another; that we cannot partner with Him without first partnering with each other.

William Shakespeare sums up romantic love in his Sonnet 116.

Let me not to the marriage of true minds
Admit impediments. Love is not love
Which alters when it alteration finds,
Or bends with the remover to remove.

O no! it is an ever-fixed mark
That looks on tempests and is never shaken;
It is the star to every wandering bark,
Whose worth's unknown, although his height be taken.

Love's not Time's fool, though rosy lips and cheeks
Within his bending sickle's compass come;
Love alters not with his brief hours and weeks,
But bears it out even to the edge of doom.

If this be error and upon me proved,
I never writ, nor no man ever loved.

I had to drop my *doubt* and admit to myself that here was pretty powerful stuff. I had to ask myself, "How else can there be anything more to the life of love if it...

* Removes all impediments,
* Does not shrink as the Loved One changes,
* Is challenged, but remains constant,
* Does not diminish with time,
* Is unalterable

What a powerful statement and summary about love.

But my mind kept toying with the subject. As Christians, is something more demanded of us - so that the world will know that we are Christians? What is lacking? That which cannot elevate romantic or brotherly love to the fullness of the SPIRITUAL love to which we are called by the redemptive act of Christ is its EXCLUSIVITY. That exclusivity identifies it as part of nature. To elevate love to the level of love that qualifies as Christian, it must...

1. Transcend mere chemical attraction
2. Effectively destroy the need for exclusivity, and
3. Eliminate the expectation of reciprocity.

I thought: What natural love always includes, whether conjugal or brotherly love, is the element of self-interest. It springs from a subconscious, egotistical need to possess and/or belong. Its first impulse flows from our primal need for survival, self-gratification and enhancement. These are the elements that hold it to the natural order. When we are liberated from any egotistical need, we are moving toward the exercise of Divine love... and they will know we are Christians. They will know that we are expressing, in the best way that we can, the love expressed by Jesus, Who, "though

He was by nature God, did not consider His rank in the Godhead something to be clung to. Rather, He emptied Himself," That is, He set aside the glory of his divination and it privileges, and took on human flesh, poured Himself into our fallen, wretched, human condition. He so identified with us that He was "truly human in all things, like us, except He did not sin." But He took our sins upon Himself, and laid down His life for our salvation. As one spiritual mind summed it up. "He paid a debt He did not owe, because we owed a debt we could not pay."

And so, He teaches us what love really is, divested of all egotistical germination or limitation. If the world is to know that we are Christians by our love, then we must take the virtues, the values and the behaviors generated by natural love and elevate them without judgement and discrimination to the whole of human interaction.

The life of Jesus prompts a few questions as revealed in Scripture:

* If you greet only your friends, so what?
* If you gift, and care for, and empower only your relatives and friends, so what?
* If you look out only for those who look out for you, so what?

Even the pagans, the unbelievers, do as much. What Jesus said is this: YOUR love must be like that of the Father's. "He lets His sun shine and His rain fall on good and bad alike." There is no partiality. There is no discrimination in His sharing of love. How do we

34

Christians cultivate such impartiality? First, we must ask, "Who are we really and what really is the seed, the root, the trunk, the limb, and the blossom of this Christian reality? Oh yes, we go faithfully to church. We pool our resources to build beautiful buildings in which to worship our God. But scripture tells us: "The heavens proclaim the glory of God, and the earth shows forth His handiwork." In other words, the whole of creation is the Church of God and is a place of worship with humans as caretakers. As for the temples we build, "There will not be left a stone upon a stone." Interestingly, Jesus was the son of a carpenter. Yet there is no scriptural evidence that He ever held a hammer to pound a nail. There is no record that He built houses of worship. Rather, he used all his energy - even to shedding the last drop of His blood - "to elevate and embellish the temples not made with hands." You, I, the entire human community - we are the temple of God, the temple not made by hands. And it is in us that the Spirit of God truly resides.

When we get serious about building and embellishing the temples not made with hands - doing whatever it takes to actualize all the unique potential that God has placed in each person - then we will be living a life of love by which "they will know that we are Christians."

St. Paul, in his first epistle to the Corinthians, Chapter 13:1-13, elevates love from primary school to high school: "If I speak in the tongue of men or of angels, but do not have love, I am only a resounding gong or a clanging cymbal." This chapter bears re-reading, at least weekly, as we go about our lives in the marketplace of the world.

Jesus, before he goes out to die for us, takes the subject of love to graduate school. In His final priestly prayer, He had already given His followers final instructions. Then He prayed for them that they all would come to realize their unity. Only then would they know the fullness of love - demanded by the First Commandment: "You are to love the Lord your God with your whole mind, and all your strength...and your neighbor as yourself." However, there was the one who tried to trip Him up so that he could feel justified in wiggling his way out of this universalization of Christian love. He asked Jesus, "Well, sir, just who is my neighbor?" At this point Jesus tells the story of the "Good Samaritan." Conclusion: our neighbor is anyone who is in need. Attend to the needs of all, without exception. Why? Because all are made in the image and likeness of God. The one Divine nature of God is constituted in three Divine persons. Likewise, the one human nature is constituted in the whole of humanity. And because there is only one Divine nature, we believe the revelation given by the prophet: "Hear, O Israel, the Lord your God is one God." And God said "Now let us create beings in Our image." He made one nature, human, and individualized it in a plurality of persons. He did not do this to set up a hierarchy or a power structure within this creation. In fact, He warned, "Who would aspire to be the greatest among you must become the servant of all." No. This massive individualization and diversity were to give visible expression to His infinite creativity. Nevertheless, as a by-product of our fall from grace, and as human beings have multiplied and dispersed over the long history of time, we developed geographical and sociological constructs, binding ourselves together in these constructs, and thereby, losing our sense of the unity of our common humanity.

Jesus, knowing that His ministry was drawing to a close and knowing what had to be done to restore us to the original creative intent of God, prayed to His Father: "Father, I pray, that they all may be ONE, as You are in Me, and I in You. May they also be one in Us, so that the world will know that You have sent Me."

This prayer sums it up for the Christian. Baptized into Christ Jesus, we are called to identify with Him, His person, and His mission. Listen to some sociological constructs that we too often use to define and divide "us" vs. "them" - Color, Ethnicity, Gender, Nationality, Religion, even DNA.

I took a look at my life and gave a name to that little portion of humanity with which I identify and asked myself, "Why these walls?" The poet, Robert Frost, said, "Something there is that doesn't love a wall…that wants it down." That Something that wants no walls is the Divine spark - like flint on steel - struck at the moment God created human nature. That Something is Oneness. We are all One in Him. If One, then we must give to every human encounter the acceptance, the love, the courtesy, the care that we would give to Him, the Christ, and that we want for ourselves. This is bringing love to the point of transformation, initiating us into the very family of God.

As we hunger for the return of Christ and the fullness of our redemption, Revelation is screaming to us: "all creation…all creation…is waiting for our revelation as sons and daughters." Waiting, that is, for us to break out of our isolation, our egotistical self-interest, and to work earnestly for the actualization of the potential of every human person that comes into our lives as we are willing to work for our own fulfillment and those whose chemical attraction has ensnared us or those who comprise the sociological constructs that we claim defines our identity.

What does that mean when we encounter a homeless person hallucinating, a road rage, an unfriendly or uncaring store clerk, a Democrat or Republican who refuses to listen to our views? We must shine the light and love that Christ offered to all. We must do this in ALL of our interactions - and really believe it and feel it.

Then by this love and only then will they know that we are Christians.

"The blind will see;
the lame will walk;
the dead will rise;
and the poor will have the
Good News preached to them."

5   Just-In-Case Faith

I pondered: Where can we, lowly fallen creatures that we are, find the Will of God? Jesus answers: "I am the Way, the Truth, and the Life." Every person who seeks to inherit a place in the Kingdom lives by *Faith*.

The real challenge of human life, then, and the call of Baptism is one of Faith in the Divine Source of all life. But the paradox of Faith is that it is at once both darkness and light. St. John of the Cross suggests that the blinking light of Faith plunges us into the "dark night of the soul." The mystery of this paradox is that the brighter the light, the deeper the darkness; and the deeper the darkness, the brighter the light. What is this darkness that is also light? Maybe this darkness is the real paradox that we call the light of Faith. No wonder the question of Faith often creates confusion. A state of confusion is a kind of darkness. However, the confusion that is a quality of Faith is not a debilitating but a motivating kind of darkness. It keeps pushing us always forward in hopes of finding the light. HOPE, then, is a dynamo that energizes the journey of true Faith. If we want to bring Faith to the realm of the rational, we must first annihilate the determination that reason has to acquire certainty. "Because you say 'I see,'" Jesus warned the Pharisees, "you shall die in your sin."

Faith, then, seems to be a fundamental but often elusive virtue, one that can be derailed easily by a posture of certainty. This may be at the very crux of our collapsing societal morality and civilized discourse.

Jesus asked this question of His Apostles: "Think you that the Son of man will find Faith on the earth when He comes again?" It was not an idle question, for the more society advances in science and technology, the greater is the tendency to fall away from the "habit" of Faith. And the more we become mesmerized by our own inventions and conclusions, the further away we are drawn from the practice of internal reflection, the joy of solitary contemplation and the personal growth and spiritual expansion that results from interpersonal relationships. This stands in opposition to frenzied Facebook friending, intemperate tweeting, and app-land addiction. The end result of all these distractions is that we are led by our own contrivances to move further away from the personality expansion and enrichment that can only grow from internal reflection and communion with the Divine Guest waiting silently and patiently in that Kingdom that is within us. Faith and the questions surfaced by it are pushed to the back burner. They no longer take center stage.

Yes, some of the "would-be Faithful" do keep going through the motions of religious practices and the pretense of personal piety. They may still declare in private musings and public discourse that they are people of Faith. But what kind of Faith is it? Is it the Faith that Jesus assured us would move mountains, or is it "just-in-case" Faith?

Some of us Christians want so desperately to know God. We really do. We want to love God with our whole heart. We want to serve God with all our strength. We call ourselves people of Faith, and we participate, more or less, in practices designed to express that Faith; but when we honestly examine our hearts, when we critically evaluate our works, we find many reasons to wonder if we truly are people of Faith; if, in fact, we really do believe. Of course, we say we do. Sometimes, we are even sure we do. In the case of Clergy, why else would they involve themselves in a life of public ministry? Why else would they celebrate Eucharist, making new Jesus' Paschal experience, the mysterious reenactment of our deliverance from the slavery of sin and death to liberation, resurrection, and life? Why else, if they do not believe?

But the question lingers: Is ours the Faith that St. Paul defines? Does ours have that quality of "confident assurance concerning what we hope for, the conviction about things which we do not see." Would we have walked on water? We must ask if ours is that Faith spoken of by Jesus who assured us that if it were even only the size of a mustard seed, we could say to the mountain, "Be lifted from your place and hurled into the sea, not doubting, and it would be done."

That kind of Faith carries with it tremendous power. In the eleventh chapter of the Epistle to the Hebrews, the sacred writer delineates examples of that power, examples that we know so well:

• Abraham's journey and the call to sacrifice his son,
• Sarah's pregnancy in her old age,
• Noah and his Arc that survived the flood,
• Moses and the parting of the Red Sea,
• Joshua and the collapse of the walls of Jericho.

42

The writer goes on with many more examples until, exhausted, he says, "Time won't let me tell you all of the wonders accomplished by Faith." These were wonders that allowed those believers to redeem themselves and their times. Few though they were, they achieved much because they had the *confident assurance* concerning what they hoped for, a *firm conviction* about the things that God promised, even though they were not able to see the outcome.

And what about us today? The question continues to gnaw at me. Will our Faith be strong enough to redeem our times? Here in America, our society is in a period of decline that is greater, more pervasive, and more radical than at any previous time in our history. We are a nation of over 328 million people, the majority of whom say, "I believe." We have more of us saying "I believe," than any other nation in the Western world. And of that percentage who say "I believe," the majority claim to be Christians, declaring publicly that "Jesus is the Lord of my life and of all life."

Yet, despite our claims to still be a people of Faith, our society is awash in incidents that run counter to the works of Faith. Faith conduces to life and love, yet our rate of murder, production, and sale of weapons of death and destruction, and all forms of social violence are alarmingly high. Lying, cheating, and stealing are endemic. The acquisition of money and power are the primary goals, displacing increasing numbers of people into helplessness and hopelessness. They are collateral damage in our quest for power and wealth. Faith

43

questions no longer motivate our collective public life nor frame our social and political decisions.

In the midst of this encroaching degeneracy, the depth and quality of our Faith as individuals requires ongoing re-examination. If we are honest in this examination, we might discover that our society is collapsing around us not so much because the small percent who say they do not believe are so powerful in their lack of Faith, but rather that we, the Believers, are so weak in our expression of Faith. We might find that what we call our Faith is not the Scriptural virtue of Faith that truly sets us free; but rather a "just-in-case Faith" that keeps us in bondage.

It's not just Millennials, but also people in the pews of Christian Churches, even some of us wearing the Roman collars and the veils of vowed religion that find, in reality, we are not very sure about this Being called God. We're not very sure about this person called Christ. We're not very sure about life after death – about final accountability and judgment. We have heard it said, "Everybody wants to go to heaven, but nobody wants to die."

But Just in Case!

So, we do a few good things. Mainly, we avoid doing what we think this *Maybe God* perceives as bad – just in case. We endure the boredom of muddling through a few pious practices of our Faith. For example, we say prayers just in case; we donate a few dollars to the poor out of our excess, just in case; we refrain from violence to ourselves or others, just in case; perhaps some of us even made the decision to become vowed celibates – just in case.

What does such Faith – "just-in-case" – mean, if anything? Are we, the practitioners of such Faith, enabled to accept the wisdom of Jesus expressed in the Gospel: "Fear not, little flock…?" Are we quite sure we Just-In-Case believers, that "It has pleased the Father to give us a Kingdom?" Do we think that Jesus is being a bit extreme when He counsels: "Go sell all that you have and give the proceeds in alms to the poor?" And from this view of "just-in-case Faith," isn't Jesus demanding too much when He asks that we be always on guard, always living our lives as if we were servants waiting for the master, always watching out for the master's affairs? Not ever being concerned about our own – not even our own life? That level of commitment is too much for "just-in-case Faith."

But Real Faith impels us to the realization that Jesus could not ask less. This Jesus, "who did not consider His rank in the Godhead a privilege to be clung to, but emptied Himself and took the nature of a slave." This Jesus, who, despite the fact that all things were His, chose to be born in a stable, to grow up in obscurity, to walk with and befriend the poor, to suffer rejection and betrayal, to be broken and poured out, to shed the last drop of His blood in the suffocating and excruciating death of crucifixion. This Jesus knew full well that in order to gain all, one must surrender all. The French writer, Saint-Exupery, says it eloquently in his book, *The Little Prince*: "Perfection is achieved, not when

45

there is nothing more to add, but when there is nothing more to be taken away."

And the Bible says it this way: "Unless the grain of wheat falls into the ground and dies, it will never be anything more than a grain of wheat. But if it dies (if it surrenders all that it is and has), it brings forth much fruit."

I am wandering in the shadows.

How can we evaluate whether our Faith is just-in-case or real Faith? Five characteristics can help us discern. Maybe the answer is in the word, itself. Consider Faith as an acronym:

- Focus
- Attitude
- Insight
- Trust, and
- Healing

I think of it - at least for this moment, in this way:

F=FOCUS
Is my attention on my pleasure or God's? In my life choices, do I look to see how much I can please myself without displeasing God? Jesus reflects the person of real Faith this way. "My meat is to do the will of Him who sent Me."

A=ATTITUDE

Do I experience sacrifice primarily as pain or opportunity? Do I experience a sense of privation, intrusion, annoyance, or feel put upon when I am inconvenienced or required to make some personal sacrifice, or endure pain and suffering? Wouldn't real Faith turn such occasions into opportunities, and find in the end result a kind of internal joy despite the external cross? Jesus reflects the attitude of one with real Faith. He said, "I have a Baptism with which I am to be baptized, and how am I on fire to have it accomplished!" Yet, we know the thought of the cross itself was so painful, He sweat blood.

I=INSIGHT

Am I able to trace with any degree of assurance the guiding hand of God in the unfolding of my life? Are there any moments about which I can say, "On this or that occasion, God was really with me?" Jesus' life reflects such insight when He said, "He who sent Me is with Me and He never leaves Me because I do always the things that are pleasing to Him."

T=TRUST

Do I take the necessary actions to bring about good – not depending on outcomes, not attempting to measure or judge results, but, as the Apostle Paul advised, always planting and watering, knowing that whether I see it or not, God is giving the increase. Jesus says, "my Father works until now, and I work."

H=HEALING

Finally, are there miracles in my life? God promised that miracles would happen where there is Real Faith. But even the divine power of Jesus was stymied by "just-in-case" Faith as the Scripture writer attested, "And Jesus could work no miracles in that town because of their unbelief." Yes, real Faith is accompanied by miracles. The miracle of healing can take many forms, including in the deepest core of the self from whence springs the motivation for all that we do, gradually healing the sick and sinful condition out of which we operate so that our lives become integrated, our motivations purified, and our actions transforming. This is the greatest healing miracle brought on by Faith.

Real Faith will save us. And only with Real Faith can we hope to save our society. Only with Real Faith can we hope to bring to fruition and fulfillment that final prayer of Jesus: "I pray, Father, that they all may be ONE" : "The blind will see; the lame will walk; the dead will rise; and the poor will have the Good News preached to them."

The sacrament of Baptism establishes in us the Kingdom of God. Contemplation brings us into deep and inseparable relationship with the God of the Kingdom. From this union, I think, REAL FAITH emerges.

*"We will know Him
in the breaking
of the Bread..."*

6   Breaking

The Bread was there, and the Wine, and the cup. I was alone. Waiting. Waiting. Waiting for someone. A friend. Someone who believed in Him. Someone who longed for Him as I did. Someone who was constantly in search of Him as I was. And then we would break the Bread, as He had instructed us who believe, in memory of Him. I knew we would find Him again in some new, unexpected way, in the breaking of the Bread.

I was waiting for Him. Waiting for the world, for He is world. It is too small an image that holds Him to one historical moment, that enshrines Him in the flesh of one individual Man, or tries to channel Him through the celebration of Sacrament, scantily understood. He spans all of history. He is both Creator and Created, Producer and Product, Artist and Art. He permeates it all, the divine Leaven in the fermenting mass. But, at the same time, He is the all-embracing "Ambiente," the Mystical Milieu in which it is all held together, all contained, the Wholly Immanent, the Completely Transcendent. How audacious our attempts to define God with our self-constructed language and limited knowledge! What might He not have taken as Symbol of His presence?

Moses felt the ardent heat of Him in the burning bush, a Fire consuming, but never consumed. The Israelites found Him in the cloud that hovered over them in the desert, leading them through a chartless space, sheltering them from a blistering sun. By night, He was the Fire that warmed them, the Light that conquered their darkness. And in that dry place, He was to them a

Rock, springing living water. St Paul says very simply, "They drank from the Rock that followed them, and the Rock was Christ."

Paul learned, too, that He was a whole people called away from the temple, the old law and sacrifice; a whole people made one with Him by a new commandment of love.

> "Saul, Saul, why are you persecuting Me?"
> "Who art Thou, Lord?"
> "I am Jesus of Nazareth whom you are persecuting."

Could this really be? Had the blow he struck to a Christian heart actually wounded the Heart of Jesus? This Jesus, whom the earth had already surrendered and the heavens claimed? "I am Jesus of Nazareth whom you are persecuting."

And He is the blind, the lame, the sick, the prisoner, the rich, and the poor. He is the one who is hungry, and the one who thirsts. "I was hungry, and you gave me something to eat." Are we dumbfounded by His presence in the derelict, the destitute, the broken? They asked, "Lord, when did we see You hungry and give You food?" And He taught them about another Sacrament of His Presence. "As long as you did this to one of the very least, you did it to Me...."

Yes, He permeates it all. He contains it all. He envelops it all. The psalmist understood. He cried out:

"Where can I go from Your Spirit
From Your presence, where can I flee?
If I go up to heavens You are there
If I sink to the nether world You are present there,
If I take the wings of the dawn
If I settle at the farthest limits of the sea,
Even there, Your Hand shall guide me,
And Your right Hand hold me fast…"

So many ways He has given us to get to know Him. But they knew Him 'in the breaking of the Bread."

Why Bread? Lord, why have you chosen Bread? Is it because of the special care that goes into its making? Is it because 'Your' times, 'Your' culture, 'Your' place regarded it as the "staff of life?" Is it because the one loaf is the product of many melded grains? Is it because the sharing of bread is a sign of friendship? *Doubt* wanted to envelop me. But would He deceive a friend?

"I have *not* called you servants; I have called you *friends*." It had to be true, and suddenly I thought I knew "Why Bread?" Because the bread can never be shared without being broken?

Because it wasn't just the Bread. It was the Bread, *Broken*. "They knew Him in the *Breaking* of the Bread. Yes, there can be no bread shared until there has been bread broken.

"During the meal, Jesus took the Bread
He blessed it, broke it, and gave it to His disciples.
"Take this and eat it."

He said, "for this is My Body
Which shall be broken for you...
Do This in memory of Me."

Likewise, the *Cup*. They must drink it, this Cup, His Blood which was to be poured out, in memory of Him.

Do what in memory of Him? What was He really asking? Just eat the Bread and drink the cup? Just this, and nothing more? Or was he asking that we be *broken* and *poured out* as well? Suddenly, I was fully myself again. I had never thought of that before. Fully myself - fully aware. I spoke aloud to the Presence that now pulsated in my heart. Why have we, Lord, made so much of the eating and drinking, so much of the substance of the Bread and Wine? So much of spoken formulas and enacted rituals? And why have we built a cult, a privileged class around it? And why have we made so little of the *brokenness*? Is it not the *brokenness* and the being *poured out* that made the Sacrament, this Transubstantiation, possible for us? We for each other?

Maybe this is why the "disciple whom Jesus loved" did not even bother to record the incident. Maybe this disciple, the beloved, the one who leaned on Jesus' breast and felt the love that consumed Him pulsating in His sacred Body, maybe this disciple understood better than them all, that it was in the *brokenness* and the *being poured out* that Jesus would be present. Maybe he understood better than all the others that this Sacrament was far more inclusive than the ritualization of a memorial meal to be enacted on a wooden altar in a man-made temple by a privileged few. Maybe he knew

53

that the "Upper-room" would be, forever after, the Temple of the Spirit that is the human soul; and the Sacred Table, the Altar, would be the human heart; and the Bread of His presence would be the flesh of each human being that is broken, the blood of each human being that is *poured out* in concern for another. So, the "disciple whom Jesus loved" does not tell us about Jesus "breaking the bread," he tells us, instead, about Jesus breaking Himself. He tells us about union, about love, about service. He tells us about Jesus washing their feet and giving them a new commandment, and Jesus pleading on their behalf, baring the yearnings of His heart to the Father for them. Jesus, about to be broken. I sank back into the deep well of subconscious reflection.

The Bread was there, and the Wine. I ate the Bread and drank the Wine. And I understood that they were not quite Sacrament. Not because they hadn't been "spoken over by a privileged someone called Priest," but because I had consumed them without letting them consume me. I had not yet let myself be *broken* and *poured out* for others, in memory of Him.

Can You Watch One With Me

"Each One Reach One"

They said to one another, "Were not our hearts burning inside us as He talked to us on the road and explained the Scriptures to us?" They got up immediately and returned to Jerusalem, where they found the eleven and the rest of the company assembled. They were greeted with, "The Lord has risen..."

7   Poor in Spirit

If I have labored over this question of *doubt*, it is because I have, without really wanting to, succumbed to its allurements, found a new life in its wisdom. I first made its acquaintance as I lay prone, recuperating from illness, reflecting on my life, the things and events that had been important to me, and wondering, when it would all be totaled in eternity, what difference it would really make. The book that I had with me was the Bible. I had read it many times before, studied it in my theology classes, searched for the meaning of its obscure lines in the tiny footnotes appended to the bottom of the page by people known as exegetes.

Those had been exciting days, secure days. Armed with the interpretations of Biblical scholars and the Summa Theologica, I stood firmly on absolutely safe ground. God was Father. God the Son was incarnate in the body politic. And the Pope couldn't make a mistake. The faithful breathed with the breath of the Holy Spirit, and Revelation was finished, with John's Apocalypse. One had only to say, Amen. Everybody knew the way. The man "earned his bread by the sweat of his brow," the "woman was saved by childbearing." And all were in obedience to an infallible authority, a teaching magisterium, that sifted down from Peter's chair to the lesser thrones perched solidly over the shoulders of the "the faithful," that low on the totem pole group called the "laity" that made up "the people of God' of the local Churches.

But, then, in that now far away day, when the book lay on the stand beside my sickbed, and I opened it in search of comfort, consolation, and reassurance, it became a whole new revelation. "Blessed," the verse began, "are the poor in spirit." The poor in spirit. It was the beginning of His message. He did not say, "Blessed are the poor," but "the poor in spirit." He could not have sanctioned poverty as a state of blessedness. He was the Son of a prodigal God, an extravagant Father who lavished His creation with wealth and beauty, fingerprinting even each melting snowflake with a unique design. No, it was to be the "poor in spirit," the souls that are empty of egotism, who live in a constant, conscious need of the Lord; the souls that are stripped of all pretense, cleansed of all deceptions, who stand in the Truth; the naked soul, cocooned in silence, waiting, attentive, always tasting its need while, at the same time, relishing the sweet delicacies of the assurance that the Lord is filling it.

I had thought once of being poor. I even took a vow, but the vow never touched on much that was important. And those who taught me about the vow never taught me how to empty my heart of idle dreams and make it a ready reed for the breath of the Holy Spirit to blow through and make His melody, a new melody, a new revelation of His Presence in the world. *Poor* meant so many other things: darned stockings and patched skirts, limited baths and tiny cells. It focused on matter, not spirit. It had all sorts of guises: use things but don't own them: have what you need, but only let someone else give you permission to have it. And the new cry: "Simple lifestyle," something that nobody can define for anybody else, but that will use a small forest of paper and years of discussion in the attempt. And we will kid ourselves into believing that it's all about the Gospel.

The small community that followed the Lord needed no definitions. It didn't seem important that one worked naked, pulling his catch from the sea, while the Master wore a coat so fine that the Roman soldiers gambled for it at the time of His death, considering it too rich, too beautiful to disfigure by dividing the cloth. And yet, who would not have called Him poor? But it was not His stabled birth nor manger-cradle, nor even that, during His ministry, He had "not whereon to lay His Head." His poverty lay deeper than this. His poverty lay in the absolute, unqualified acceptance of who He was, and of the mission that was communicated to Him by the Father. Made Man, He never used His divine power to escape the consequences of that human condition. But He entrusted it all to the Father and was faithful to the divine will that transcended every other law. He was completely accepting of His Person, completely committed to His unique call.

Is this perhaps, the point that we keep missing? That not only Christ, but every human being is a unique, unrepeatable revelation of some aspect of God, and that each of these unique, unrepeatable persons has a singular destiny and mission? Is that, perhaps, why, in those quiet, mystical moments, we hear the echo of the Lord's admonition, "Call no man Father. One is Father, God. All you are brothers and sisters. And call no man Teacher." Hadn't He already said, "They shall all be taught of God." Hadn't He already said, "Neither on this mountain, nor in Jerusalem... but in Spirit and in Truth" shall you worship the Father for "The Kingdom of God is within You?"

This opened me up to the questions: How then, do we justify our hierarchies who love to sit in high places, wield power, and bind consciences? What of our "ex-cathedra" and our "teaching Magisterium?" Had He not said, "Let them all grow together until the harvest?" What then do we use as an excuse for our anathemas?

The poor spirit is an empty vessel held up for the Lord's filling.

But we argue that we have been told by Him to go into the whole world and teach what He commanded us. Indeed. And would that it be so, because He gave us only one command. A new commandment. He called it, "Love one another as I have loved you." That is what He commanded us, and oh, that we would teach it! With our tongue! With our life!

But the heart has to be empty to know that that is all there is. It has to be poor to endure the very real possibility that our dogmas are empty expressions of intellectual arrogance, our doctrines but faint sketches of momentary illusions, our liturgies vain posturing that impedes rather than assists worship. The spirit has to be poor to know that it cannot know, to experience with profound joy this intellectual darkness that becomes light for the heart.

That is why He began, "Blessed are the poor in spirit. They will realize the kingdom." They will discover the treasure of My presence within them and will labor to give it expression, and in 'this' labor they shall be taught of God. Yes, they shall be taught of God. So, Francis of Assisi, the poor little man, could dare to say, "Speak to me of no other rule...the Lord, God, has revealed to me what I must do." The truly poor, then, look to no man, no woman, no law, no rule. Their being is one of total attention to the Lord. Only they can be *obedient* because only they can truly hear the Lord.

Do we dare pursue this radical poverty? This "poverty of spirit" without which, in spite of prayer and work and Church and Sacrament, the kingdom may never be ours. Can we surrender our vain need for power, for some kind of dominance? Can we destroy the categories in which we have boxed ourselves looking for honor? Can we become the "empty reed" waiting for the breathing of the Spirit to make us a new melody to God? A unique melody?

As Francis repeated, "Speak to me of no other rule. Not of Benedict, nor Dominic, nor Basil. The Lord God has revealed to me what I must do." So, are we right in saying, "Speak to me of no other rule? Not of Benedict, nor Dominic, nor Basil, nor Francis. Lord God empty me, make me poor, that I, too, may hear only your voice. Only You tell me what I must do." Or do we see this as a selfish exaltation of arrogance? And of this, who will judge us? Jesus warned: "Thou shalt not judge," and Scripture fully exonerates us. "If your conscience does not accuse you, you have not sinned."

"St. Francis of Assisi"

Then they recounted what had happened on the road and how they had come to know Him in the breaking of the Bread...

8   Fullness

As I reached for this deeper understanding of "poverty of spirit," I was lost again in that tenuous world of unknowing! So, trapped in this new, but now, more intense meditative collage, I took the loaf, its strong weave of grains surrendered to the fermenting action that melded them, and I carried it lovingly, in my two hands outstretched. We, I and this bread, walked the covered earth to a hidden spring that trickles over an altar of rocks in tiny ribbons of ever-changing widths. When the sun strikes the gleaming rocks with its shaft of yellow rays, a shimmering band of colors rises and falls like a rainbow floating in slow motion. I stood where the trickle could bathe my bare feet. A new baptism. "One has only to bathe the feet and she is clean all over." I set the loaf gently on a flat, white stone creviced from the ribboned flow, tabernacled behind a sheen of undulating color. I eased down to my knees before the Bread. "Sacrament is an outward sign instituted by God to give grace." It is only the faintest whisper, like some timid echo from a distant hollow, no longer accessible. For what was not sign? Where was not grace? "All things were made by Him, and without Him was made nothing that was made." I contemplated the dome of sky that His fingers had painted, and His breath that blessed the leaf cluster of the eager Pasque flower as it grew out of the very base of the rocks in search of its own identity, its separate life. And, there again, were the same questions haunting me? Is not the flower Sacrament? Can it not be broken even as the Bread? Broken, uprooted? Whose intoxicating perfume overpowers the senses? Why not the rock? The rock which, even in its pebbled form, had power to slay the Philistinian giant? The rock that came to be the symbol of faith on which His Church was built? Wasn't it the rock, rejected by the builders that became the cornerstone?

The sun had reached the crevice and the Bread was ablaze. Flowers are broken to be made into bouquets and admired. And rocks are broken to be assembled into new, sheltering forms, but Bread is broken to be consumed. "Take this, all of you, and eat it." And they took it - the Twelve, the other disciples, men, women, all who had followed Him there, who had prepared the supper, who sat with Him to celebrate the Passover, not knowing that He was the Passover, who ate the Pascal meal, not knowing that He was the Pascal meal. They took the Bread. They consumed it. And then they argued over who among their number should be the greatest. They hadn't heard that He was the Bread. That He was broken, to be consumed. So, He said to them, "I am among you as a servant." The greatest is the one who is broken for you, the one who is consumed for you. "Do this in memory of Me."

Nevertheless, they ate the Bread and argued about who among themselves would be the greatest. And the argument wasn't settled even though they prayed together and went out with Him. And it still isn't settled. It has bloodied the pages of Christian history until, at last, it has been institutionalized, dogmatized, and even sacramentalized. The thrones have been secured, and those who sit upon them royally extend their hands to be kissed by their kneeling subjects.

But the Lord girded Himself with a towel and washed their feet. "Pagan kings lord it over their people… It cannot be that way with you. All you are brothers and sisters. He/She will be first who has been the servant of all, even as I am in your midst as servant. If you remember Me, you will do this. And when you do this, this work of love and service, the world will believe in Me; it will come to know that I am the Son, the ambassador of God.

Maybe it was the fault of a restless cloud, but half the loaf lay in shadow. Dare I bless it as He had done? Break it and eat it as He asked? Could I ever hope to be committed as He was? Wholly given? Consumed?

"But you are a holy priesthood, a royal nation, a people set apart to offer spiritual sacrifices…" to offer self. Therefore, dare I *not* bless it? Dare I *not* prepare myself for the stripping? Dare I *not* be consumed, burning away everything not enlivened by His Spirit! Priesting is no longer something that happens only at an altar with the ritualistic offering of a sacrifice. It is more than something made by the imposition of hands, and the blessing of fingers, and the saying of words. Jesus finished all that, shattered the veil and leveled the Temple. From then on, priesting would demand being consumed, letting all illusion die, all pragmatism, until the naked reality, the Divine Life is free in us, is all. Free, fully alive, and given.

"This is my Body which will be broken for you."

From that moment on, priesting would be mutual service in memory of the Lord. And worship would no longer be an act, a ritual, but a state of being. "Neither on this mountain nor in Jerusalem." (nor do all roads lead to Rome) for God is Spirit, and true worshippers will worship God in Spirit and in Truth. "Be still and see that I am God." Thus, He had cried out: "Father into Your Hands, I commend My Spirit," and "I do always the things that are pleasing to Him."

I reached out, and I took the bread. I blessed it, broke it and ate. And I felt the stirring of Life in me and the dying of illusions. And I knew for the first time that I was utterly alone, and yet completely a part of all Reality. I knew I was being called. I knew I was becoming whole. I knew I was Priest.

"Jesus On the Cross"

Some in the crowd who heard these words began to say, "This must be the Prophet." Others were claiming, "He is the Messiah." But an objection was raised: "Surely the Messiah is not to come from Galilee? Does not Scripture say that the Messiah, being of David's family, is to come from Bethlehem, the village where David lived?" In this fashion, the crowd was sharply divided over Him..."

John 7: 40-44

9   Thoughts

I was thinking of *doubt* again. I can't explain my present
obsession. Maybe it's because so many things that were
taught to me as I was growing up have been proven to
be false. No one group or person has a monopoly on
Truth. God's presence in our history transcends all
human ability to perceive it. By now, after so much trial
and error, we, of faith, should at least suspect that each
manifestation in creation is a refracted reflection of
some aspect of the Creator; and we stand before these
manifestations like the three blind men in their partial
and imperfect probing of the elephant. And,
unfortunately, like the blind men, we insist on defining
the whole elephant according to the small part of it that
we have managed to touch. "The elephant," exclaimed
the first blind man as he clung to the tail, "is all rope."
This poor man *did not doubt* that, in his blindness, he
might be missing something, and so he closed his mind
to his colleague at the other end who, hanging onto the
animal's cylindrical trunk, called out, "No my friend!
He is all a massive tube!"

And both these blind men were contemptuous of the
fellow between them who, running his hand along the
animal's broadside, vociferously contradicted them. "It
is right that they call you blind!" he scoffed. "It is
obvious to anyone with the least sensitivity of touch;
that the elephant is a great wall."

So we, through our constant *doubt* of the limited insight
and fallible testimony that grow out of the human
experience, combined with our constant effort to put
69

these limited pieces together so as to attain a little more of the Truth, may finally touch that Wisdom Incarnate which is Christ, who wrote on no tablets of stone, developed no theological systems, set up no hierarchies to judge and rule. His admonition to Peter was to "feed" not *rule* His lambs, His sheep. And his commission to His Apostles was to "teach what I have commanded you. "What He commanded them, of course, was that they "love one another as I have loved you."

It was this life of love that counted. It was not dogma, not doctrine, not sacraments, not liturgy, not traditions, not laws, not authority. It was *this life of love* alone that would make them credible witnesses; the wisdom of love, not that of logic, that would lead them to truth.

And so, St. Paul concluded: "And there remains faith, hope, and charity – these three – but the GREATEST of these is CHARITY!"

The sun rested on the horizon like a mounted jewel in an ancient temple. And the Son rested on the mountain in the prayer that rose to His Father. And while He was praying, His face changed in appearance and His clothes became dazzling white. Suddenly, two men were talking with Him – Moses and Elijah. They appeared in glory and spoke of His passage which He was about to fulfill in Jerusalem. Peter, and those with him, had fallen into a deep sleep; but awakening, they saw His glory and likewise saw the two men who were standing with Him. When they were leaving, Peter said to Jesus, 'Master, how good it is for us to be here. Let us set up three altars: one for You, one for Moses, and one for Elijah.' (He did not know what He was saying.) While he was speaking, a cloud came and overshadowed them, and the disciples grew fearful as the others entered it. Then from the cloud came a voice which said, 'This is my Son, My chosen One. Listen to Him.' Then, lifting their eyes, they saw only Jesus, for He was there now all alone. Then Jesus strictly bade them, 'Tell the vision to no one until the Son of Man be risen from the dead!'"

10   In Him

The sun rested on the horizon like a mounted jewel on the high altar of an ancient temple. And the Son rested on the mountain. And the disciples looking up saw only Jesus. Moses and Elijah had disappeared into the cloud. God's chosen people had completed the work that He had set them apart to do. They were to look to no one now, but only Jesus. Shortly after the Transfiguration incident, He would be mounted on the Cross, and His death cry would rend asunder the Temple Veil.

The Temple worship had come to an end. "Neither on this Mount, nor in Jerusalem...." He had become the temple. "Destroy this Temple, and in three days, I shall raise it up." As for that other Temple..." Not a stone shall be left upon a stone." And He had become the altar. "No one goes to the Father except by way of Me." And He had become the sacrifice. "Behold the Lamb of God...Behold Him who takes away the sins of the world." And He was the new High Priest. "Thou art a priest forever according to the Order of Melchizedech."

The Apostles knew that it was finished with and in Him. They never called themselves priests. They were town criers, harbingers of the Good News that Christ had come, had died, had risen and would come again. The human family had but to put their faith and trust in Him.

The incarnation of Jesus had "Christ-ed" the whole world. All things were sacred. All creation was sacrament. All humans of faith were priests.

His new law was far more comprehensive than all the prescriptions of the old law taken together. From that moment on, the great sin would be desacralization, for this meant working against the action of the "Spirit" of Jesus alive, always alive, and moving in His Creation. How could anything not be holy when, as Scripture attests, "All things were made by Him; and without Him was made nothing that was made,"? I had to ponder. What was the conclusion if this, indeed, is true? With His *law of love* had not Christ called us to a task of de-compartmentalization of Reality? Had He made all Reality one sacred whole? Had He made all Reality sacrament?

Could *Profane* as opposed to *sacred* ever again be anything more than a logical construct? Did it not make a statement only about the *user* of Reality, not about Reality itself? The Humanist says, "Because I am human, nothing human is alien to me." The Believer, the true Christian, says, "Because I am Christian, nothing created is profane to me, because I truly understand that 'all things were made by Him; and without Him was made nothing that was made...'" "And lifting up their eyes, they saw none other, but Jesus alone."

"Mother's Love"

In His Image

In His Image…
That's what God said.
And how the phrase has haunted me ~
I, this thing of broken flesh ~
Image Him!
How can this be?

And so my brokenness I loathed
Until His echo in my soul
Traversed its very breath and length,
"O, Little One,
How would you
But in your weakness
Know my strength?"

I grasped to break my fallen state
And clutched the empty air.
I would have plunged eternally
Except His sheltering arm was there,
"O, Little One,"
But for your fall
You would not know my love at all."

SO - In wounded flesh and fallen state
Through gentle nurturing of His grace
And shadowy glimpses of His face
I heard him whisper loud and clear
"To mirror Me, this is your part,

GO - Take my world in your embrace
And heal its broken heart."

Black Woman

I am Black but beautiful
O ye daughters of Jerusalem
As the tents of Kedar
As the curtains of Salmah
Do not regard me lightly
Because of my darkness...

11 Blackness

Really? Is there really a genetic superiority among the different groups in the human community determined by skin pigmentation? There is reason for doubt. In fact, it seems to be the most stupid idea that ever went through a human brain. But where is the proof?

As I see it – the sun sifting through the leaves under which I sat, she was young and Black and beautiful. Her skin was a sheen of velvet that she refused to dull with cosmetics. Her hair was soft, natural, cropped short and carefully groomed, a halo for her head. Her eyes were wide open, alive and daring. Her full lips were ripe for loving. The movement of her body was free-flowing like a playful wind. And she tingled with nervous energy, anxious for life. But there were times when her being slipped into an unnatural rigidity, taut like a startled deer alerted to danger.

Before her, there was the mother. Her face was a furrowed field; her hands, a mountain of callouses. The strands at the temples of her forehead had grayed much too early. Her pressed hair lay flat against her head, except at the very edges where the daily sweat of existence kept alive in her the deposit of a larger truth.

After her, there was the child, flaunting her braided hair that ended in the captivity of silk red ribbons. Her body was scantily clad, her thin limbs freed from the oppress of clothing. With bare feet, she leaped gingerly over the lines that broke the sidewalk into separate squares. The primal consciousness was still alive in her that warned, "Whatever breaks the unity is bad."

Black Women All!
What does it mean, this Blackness? This rich, rich symbol that encapsulates all the primal colors of the universe with their myriad shades and hues and tones, and blends them, with reverence, in its tissues and its pores? Is it really a *void*, as society would have us believe? An *emptiness*? Something *base*? A symbol of *nothingness*? A condition of the flesh to be *despised*?

All creation is, in some respects, a mirror of Divinity. Any positive spirituality begins with this awareness and the subsequent appreciation that this awareness evokes. *Darkness* is a negative symbol only for those who have touched the Divine Mystery in only the most superficial of ways, if at all. For those who have delved deeper, who have uncovered, little by little, the multiple layers of the unconscious, who have experienced, through the gradual diminishment of passing strength, the very real fragility of the human condition, who have reverently touched, in the lull of sensory experience, the Divine Reality dwelling in the deep, inner void, in the dark center of being; for those, Blackness is the sweet, ripe symbol of that persistent invitation on the part of God that we mere mortals enter with Him into the fullness of Life.

Reality being what it is, the Black Woman, in touch with her very real dignity, is not diminished by society's assessment of herself as the symbol of the *void*. For it is in the *void*, in the emptiness, that God finds the playground for His creative power. It was so in the beginning. The author of Genesis tells us:

In the beginning (when there was nothing but emptiness)
God created the heavens and the earth.
The earth was a formless *void*.
And the deep presided in *darkness*.
And God's Spirit hovered over the waters....

And the people of God pray in testimony, "As it was in the beginning, is now, and ever shall be."

And society would have the Black Woman wear her darkness with shame. But it was in the dark, empty space of the Woman's Womb that God's Spirit worked the miracle of the Incarnation, preparing for the insertion of Himself into human history. And society would have the Black Woman temper her Blackness, make it less conspicuous, tone it down. But it was in the *blackness* of a blessed night that the herald announced the birth of a Savior.

And the people of God pray in testimony, "As it was in the beginning, is now, and ever shall be." For still the Savior comes in darkness, St John of the Cross would say, "...in the dark night of the soul."

Reality being such as it is, the Black Woman, in touch with her very real dignity, is not denigrated by the popular concept of *blackness* as a symbol of something *base*, as *nothingness*, as a condition to be *despised*. For she knows from the witness of the Apostle, Paul, that

80

such interpretation only demonstrates a lack of inner understanding, a profound ignorance. Even more, she knows that such an interpretation only enhances her "favored position" in the eyes of the Lord. St. Paul writes: (and I translate his thought into today's idiom) "… Those whom the powerful of this world hold in low esteem, whom they regard as worthless, whom they cast aside as nothing - these are the very ones that God chooses in order to point out their blindness and their lack of wisdom…."

Blackness, then, is in the world as a symbol of the reality of the one truly essential human vocation which is to make within the spaces of human being and environment a meeting place for union with the Divine. In the absence of response to this call, all other human activity is ultimately meaningless. It is the symbol of that primal wisdom in the created being that makes no claims, that strips away all pretentions, that holds the human psyche in an unperturbed attitude of waiting. It is the symbol of the void that perpetually seduces the Divine Being to continue the Creative Process until the fullness of Life has been reached.

There is no coming to the Light for anyone who has not embraced the Darkness. There are no Stars for those who fear the Night.

The Black Woman, precisely because of her Blackness, is God's richest symbol, for she personifies in her very being the epitome of that created wisdom which makes possible the glorious interplay between God and His Creation.

The *Song of Solomon* says it well. This canticle is an extended poetic metaphor of God in love with His Creation. In the metaphor, Creation is represented as a beautiful Woman. The following lines, situated as they are at the very onset of the Canticle, point out in poignant fashion, the symbolic function of the Black Woman as the archetype of Creation in a humanity pursued by a loving God.

The Woman Speaks:
    "...I am Black and beautiful
        O ye daughters of Jerusalem
    As the tents of Kedar
        As the curtains of Salmah,

Do not regard me lightly
        Because of my darkness...
    I am the flower of Sharon
        A lily of the valley...

And her Love, her Lord, responds:

    As a lily among thorns
        So is my beloved among women
    Rise, my beloved, my beautiful one,
        And come!

"God alone has the power
to create life;
God alone should have the right
to destroy it."

12   Trust

The nation had not completely settled down from the shake-up that followed the Civil Rights battles of the sixties which led to the extension of legal protection for Blacks, in the Civil Rights Act of 1968, before it was threatened with once more being split asunder just five years later, in 1973, in the *Roe v. Wade* decision which took legal protection away from the unborn in the first trimester of gestation. For the first time in the nation's history, private citizens, outside the consideration of self-defense, would be given the legal right to destroy the life of another. It was a wrenching decision that propelled the nation into a struggle akin to civil war. The battle lines are drawn in public debates, marches, demonstrations, threats, and even bombings. So polarized is the nation, so large the issue, so heated the emotions it engenders, that families are split asunder and political fortunes, no matter the other merits of a candidate, can be made or destroyed on this single issue alone.

At the core of the conflict is a clash of rights: the woman's right to privacy, her control over her own body, versus the right of the fetus to life and protection until it can exist independently of the woman's womb.

The conflict is packaged euphemistically as pro-choice or pro-life. The pro-life people are those who are seen as willing to trample on the rights of women, as willing to reduce the woman to nothing more than a vessel for the gestation of the male seed, as indifferent to the health and life of women. The pro-choice people are viewed as those who are willing to commit or condone murder, those who will allow women to place whatever selfish personal choices above that of the right of something so important as human life to survive. To pro-lifers, pro-choicers are destroyers of human life at its most vulnerable: the child in the womb. To pro-choicers, pro-lifers are destroyers of human rights at their most fundamental: a woman's right to control how her own body will be used.

The rending of the nation that occurred during the Civil Rights Movement resulted in the treatment of a sore that had festered too long in the body politic and the excising of which promised to lead to greater national health. The abortion issue, however, no matter what the law, threatens only to deepen the nation's wounds and lead to greater national illness.

Of course, *Roe v. Wade* did not create the abortion issue. Abortion had a way of touching many lives long before the issue was a matter of generalized public debate. In my own life, abortion touched me for the first time when, as a preschooler, I overheard the gossip of nosey neighbors critical of my mother: "I thought she'd die with Sandra. Wouldn't you think she'd quit now? One day, one of those pregnancies will take her away from here. And she won't let me help her get rid of any of them." My mother's response to suggestions that she start aborting was simple and direct. "God alone has the power to create life; God alone should have the right to destroy it." It was my first poignant lesson in "respect for life," Nevertheless, with four subsequent births that followed my own, I lived in quiet fear of my mother's possible impending death.

Abortion touched my life when I was in elementary school, and the teenage daughter of a neighbor lay dying from a botched attempt of a butcher to help her abort an unwanted fetus, conceived out of wedlock. The story was that she died from pleurisy brought on by eating green apples. But we kids, somehow, all knew. Later, the grown folks recounted how her life ebbed away while she continued to cry out, "I don't want to die! I don't want to die!"

During my years as a teaching Franciscan nun, abortion would touch my life more than once in the lives of some unmarried women. Their anguish would become my anguish; their pain, my pain.

On many occasions, because of my celibate life-style, my empathy was held suspect. Yet celibacy, far from alienating me, had more greatly sensitized me to the problem, for the life of celibacy had moved me beyond preoccupation with the particularities of my own private concerns and passions. It had drawn me ever deeper into the pains and burdens of the total human experience. Indeed, it was this growing awareness of our human solidarity that enabled me to choose the life of celibacy in the first place.

Still, on more than one occasion, my attempts to enter the abortion debate have been rejected on the grounds that my life-style made me unqualified. It is testimony to the profundity of our estrangement from one another that we have come to view the individuation implied by personhood and the social categories achieved through vocation/career differentiation as sufficient to rupture the commonality and unity of the human experience. Too little of the abortion debate is cast in this larger context. Rather, much is tied to the "legality" and "personal privacy and individual rights." Much is tied to the question of "planned parenthood" for reasons of economics, personal convenience, career choices, or the merits of abortion as a method of birth control. Much is made of the manner in which the pregnancy occurred: rape and/or incest, because people tend to feel they are more justified in destroying the fetus. Much is made of the age of the impregnated woman or the threat the pregnancy portends to her health and/or life.

And something, too, is made of the condition of the fetus. But very little, if any, of the debate is based on the reality of our *common human vocation*. So far have we destroyed in our consciousness the awareness of our unity, or our oneness, of our interrelatedness and interdependence in this experience of shared human life that we can decide that the destruction of human life, whether in potentiality or already actualized, can be regarded as a personal and private matter of choice.

All issues that impact upon the question of *life* are interconnected and must be viewed in a larger context than the mere legal question of individual rights. Issues affecting *human life,* at whatever level, are issues of moral and ethical magnitude and necessarily transcend conventional law. And when viewed from this perspective, the general common good is a far weightier imperative than the perceived rights of the individual. What stands in the way of our sympathy for this point of view is the ever-growing secularization of our social decisions. Under the pretext of favoring no religion, we have moved from being "one nation under God" to being a disconnected plurality of rugged individuals in pursuit of private, material gain at the expense of the good of the whole.

In the divine dispensation, it would seem that God's highest creative action was to bring into existence beings in the divine image through whom the glory of that divinity could be extended into visible creation. For as the divine nature is the source of unity in the trinitarian Godhead, so human nature, comprising as it does all the elements of which the visible and invisible creation is composed, becomes the source of unity of all creation. Therefore, the Incarnation Event, whereby the divine nature is joined to human nature, allows for the possibility of all creation to be subsumed once more to the Source from whence it came. This position of human nature, special and lofty as it is, nevertheless is not without serious consequences, for it negates in the individual human being the possibility of purely private action. Whatever the seeming privacy of human behavior, it is socialized to impact on humanity as a whole. This is the reality that made possible our inheritance of death through the disobedience of our first parents and our restoration to *life* through the obedience of the Savior. Between these two special primal vocations, and demonstrated by them, is the principle of solidarity that governs all human behavior. Therefore, couching the abortion debate in questions relating to "privacy" or "individual rights" is to guarantee the "abortion" of any solution related to it.

The final question to be explored, then, is what makes human life so important to God? In writing of God, St John says, "In Him was *Life*," and in writing of the creation of the human species, the author of Genesis says, "He breathed into them the *Breath of Life*." This Breath of Life implied something more than simply raising to an organic state the dust out of which humanity was created. The organic state already existed in creation. Simple evolution was sufficient for its perpetuation. This Breath of Life then, was something more. It was something akin to that Life in God alone, referred to by St. John, for Genesis continues: "and man [the human person] became a *living soul*." And it is precisely this that makes human life so important to God, for it exists to be a receptacle for the extension of divine life beyond the Godhead itself. That is why the Mother of Jesus, greeted by the Angel as "full of grace" (that is, filled with the Breath of God's Life), could respond in all humility, "My soul magnifies the Lord!"

In this transcendent scenario, the creation and nurturing of human life becomes the highest of all human vocations because it makes possible the "magnification" of the Life of God beyond the Godhead. The logical conclusion, then, is that the abortion of human life may be one of the most detestable of all human acts.

However, the problem of abortion should not be limited to a discussion of the unborn fetus, which is partially a question related to the quantification of human life, but must be extended to embrace the quality of all human life from conception to death. Every human being who deliberately acts to frustrate the realization of another person's full human potential is an abortionist. Hence, all aggression, abuse, racism, sexism, and whatever other truncating behavior, all places the perpetrator in direct opposition to the divine will, for in a truncated personality, the "Divine Life" cannot be fully magnified.

Therefore, a nation in which the destruction of human life, at whatever stage of development, is accepted, a nation in which things are valued over persons, a nation that caters to the whims of individuals without regard for the common good, a nation that disavows responsibility for the quality of life of its citizens, a nation that does not protect the weak and the vulnerable, such a nation, for its part and its purposes, may attest as does ours, "In God we trust;" but God, for His part and His purposes, cannot trust in such a nation.

Doubt leads to the search for deeper truths. Little by little, as we probe, we uncover more and more. As with the symbol of Blackness, so to, the truth about "woman's place" may be far different from what the popular conception would have us believe. Is woman really the secondary being? The mere "helping hand" to the male? The Traditionalists that maintain this position make selective use of the Bible in order to support their arguments. Who has not heard them all? Is what they offer all there is? Perhaps, there are reasons for doubt.

Annunciation

In the darkness, soft and sweet
In the lonely still of night
She felt God's breathings in her soul
The warm embrace of His Light.

The invitation whispered low
Through Angelic voice, the words were said,
"Hail, full of grace, O chosen one
I'm from your God; be not afraid."

Oh, what ecstasy to know
The meaning of the truth he'd tell
That "He from whom all life did flow
Would have her give Him life as well!"

Still wondering how such could occur,
In Faith, she gave her gentle, "Yes,"
The Spirit overshadowed her.
And there, in Virgin Earth untrod
She made a Father of her God!

13 Woman

So, maybe there are greater profundities to think about regarding this question of Woman! I moved away from shadows that so often sparked my thoughts and threw my whole consciousness into that breaking Light that blinded me to past obscurities. "Mary," I whispered, "Help me!" Then, in the recesses of my heart, I saw her there, basking in that same liberating Light that gave Life to the darkness.

Once upon a time, there was Man
And he stood before the high altar
And pleaded for the Woman
And she said, "Amen."

Once upon a time, there was Man
And he stood before the great podium
And preached to the Woman
And she said, "Amen."

Once upon a time, there was Man
And he laid his hand upon the Woman's head
And designated a place for her
And she said, "Amen."

Then the Man dismissed the Woman
For he had more "important" things to do
While the Woman remained in her assigned place
Saying all the while, "Amen."

I suspect that what comes next will be deemed provocative and a sure-to-be challenged proposition, namely, that, despite appearances, there is no shortage of priests in the Ecclesial Community, for the whole Ecclesial Community, through Baptism into the person of Christ, is inheritor of the fullness of His mission. We, Catholics, distinguish ordained priesthood from non-ordained membership in the Body of Christ and confine priesthood to the male gender. Meanwhile, signs point to our Church's ordination of women as priests within the next 50 years.

Societal trends, which too often have strongly influenced theological ideation within Religions, include the ordination of women as pastoral leaders in the following major U.S. religious traditions:

- American Baptist Church
- Buddhist
- Episcopal Church
- Evangelical Lutheran Church in America
- Jewish Reform and Conservative Movements
- Presbyterian Church (USA)
- United Church of Christ
- Unitarian Universalist
- United Methodist Church
- Pentecostal Church of God
- Assemblies of God
- African Methodist Episcopal
- Disciples of Christ
- Christian Science
  Some of them have overcome.

Currently, sadly, sexual scandal is at the forefront of issues in the Catholic Church today. Is the ordination of women as deacons less scandalous and perhaps also less controversial than the ordination of women as priests? No matter our position, I think we have to be realistic, prayerful, honest, open, and faithful as we seek the Will of God in these new and, sometimes, uncomfortable changes in our lifetime.

As we know, one important job of a priest is to listen. Pope Francis modeled this when he assigned the Study Commission on the Women's Diaconate in 2016 to be comprised of 12 members, including an equal number of men and women. He has done so again, proving that, for the truly faithful, the pursuit of Truth and Justice will not go away. So, I would like to share with you the view of ordination of women from my own reflections.

First, let's look at the story of humanity's fall from grace. Whether we put the blame on Adam or Eve is immaterial. This is a case in which, for sure, "It took two to tango." No matter how you internalize the story – whether as history, myth, parable, allegory, or whatever literary form – the theme, so to speak, the lesson to be taken from the story, puts the woman in the upper position. The Hebrew name for Adam derives from "earth," a reference and reminder that Adam was formed from the dust of the earth. The Hebrew name for Eve means "to breathe" or "to live," thus the nomenclature "mother of all the living." Here, already, is a foreshadowing of the Incarnation. To further substantiate Eve in this dominant position before the fall, we need but reflect on the punishment that resulted from their disobedience. Eve is the first to be sentenced and receives the weightier punishment. Her role in bringing life into the world would be painful. Her desire would be for her husband, and he would lord it over her. To Adam, God only said, get to work and earn a living. No more free-loading on the fruits of paradise. "You shall earn your bread by the sweat of your brow."

So, this dominant and now privileged position for the male is a punishment for sin, and our perpetuation of it is a perpetuation of the disorder *caused* by sin. But God made it clear to the woman that though she was being thusly punished, it would not remain forever. His plan for her, as mother of all the living, would be made manifest in a unique and glorious way. As a woman had initiated the fall, so a woman would birth the Redeemer. "I will put enmity between you and the Serpent [that is, the embodiment of evil], between your seed and his seed." Her seed was to include the Son of God.

Think of this, and then let's look at Ordination. What power do we say the ordained priest has over all other members of the Ecclesial Community? To work the miracle of Transubstantiation. That is, to change purely natural substance into the Body and Blood of the Living God, Jesus. Jesus used the substance of bread and wine to make His incarnated divinity ongoing in the Ecclesial Community. But bread and wine were not the *first* all-natural, material substance to undergo such a profound supernatural substantial change. If we say this power must be the exclusive prerogative of male priests ordained by the Church authority, there may be a snafu: The Virgin Mary. She was petitioned by God to allow the first act of transubstantiation to happen by offering her own flesh and blood for this purpose. This can be perceived as an action of God that is repudiated by Church authority. It is a "no thank you" to God for God's way of bringing humans their greatest and Divine Gift. Mary gave her unqualified consent, and her body is the first natural substance used by God to affect the Incarnation. And her womb is the first chalice to cradle and nurture Divine Life.

What can be concluded from this? First, the name Eve was more than just a name; it was a prophecy. Second, since God used Mary for the first incident of transubstantiation, Mary becomes the first priest ordained by God, Himself, to initiate the new order of redemption. Third, the subjugation of women resulting from the fall of grace when God said "Your desire shall be for your husband and he will lord it over you" was obviously repealed. Fourth, Mary's "YES" put her in the highest state of perfection of which humanity is capable. Her life was a full and final affirmation to this reality: "My soul magnifies the Lord." And so, she surrendered her life to God's Will: "Behold the Handmaid of the Lord; be it done unto me according to His Word." Fifth, as a result of the surrender, her own bodily substance became the first gift of nature to this unique, powerful event known as Transubstantiation, "The word was made Flesh and dwelt among us."

Mary is the first priest of the new order of salvation, ordained by God to this primacy and elevated by God to the role of "Mediatrix of all graces," bringing to fulfillment His promise to put enmity between woman and the forces of evil. Mary is indisputably the first priest of the new order, ordained by God, Himself. She becomes Mother of the Equal Rights Amendment movement in the Ecclesial Community. But societies have never accepted this re-evaluation of women to the equality expressed in the first creation story. Disregarding all the evidence of woman's ascendancy, globally, men have clung to the throne erected for them by sin. Even the Church has bought into this disorder and continues to ignore the reversal achieved by the incarnation. From humanity's fall from grace and throughout all recorded history to modern times, men have structured society to maintain themselves in postures that message them to be superior to women. But it was not meant to be permanent.

The Incarnation was God's plan for restoring the original order, and He placed a woman at the apex of this new creation. In the womb of the Virgin Mary, Divine and human life were merged, and humanity became a new creation. And Jesus, the first born of the new creation, was careful to include women in all the work and power that He would pass on to the Ecclesial Community to make His Incarnation a never-ending event. God called Woman to partner with Him in restoring the possibility for humanity to achieve the final goal for which He created it. And Jesus who declared, "Behold, I have come to do Your Will, O God," did not allow the sin-driven direction of disordered society to influence His ministerial vocation. In His movement, He brought Women back to the high profile expressed in God's creative act: "Let us make humanity in Our Own Image, after Our Own Likeness. Male and female, He made it."

I repeat, there was no inequality suggested in the original creation story, and Jesus, sent by God to restore the Divine Creative prerogative would not be influenced by the deviation resulting from the fall. And so, the Church, posturing against the restored order in a chauvinistic stance, in the case of women, has maintained its affinity with fallen society as an obstruction to the full distribution of the redemptive graces brought to the human community through the Incarnation of Jesus. As such, in relation to women, just as requiring those admitted to priesthood to be and remain unmarried, the Church has set itself up to curtail or even repudiate the restorative and liberating action of Jesus toward women.

But Jesus came to inform and reform society – not to continue to propagate the deformation wrought by sin. And so, He made sure that in His movement the sentence against women would be annulled. The original plan of God for Oneness and equality was once more in effect. And so as we read in Revelation, Chapter 12:

> "A great sign would appear in the heavens
> As Woman, adorned with the sun
> Standing on the moon
> And with the twelve stars
> On her head for a crown
> And she was pregnant and in labor
> Crying aloud in pangs of childbirth."

For through her, God was breathing His Spirit anew into His human creation. And the Woman clothed with the sun, bathed in the light, surrendered her flesh and blood for the humanization of God. With the enfleshing of Divinity, all humanity was lifted up in this Being, Christ, from its fallen state. The Spirit's Breath, the Father's Word was humanly infused by the natural substance in the Womb of a woman, and she birthed Light into a darkened world. From that moment, God demonstrated and fulfilled His promise of redemption and restoration of the human species – both men and women – to a place in His Kingdom, and His Kingdom to a place in them. The Woman's Seed broke the reign of sin, annulled the law that it generated, dispelled the darkness, and brought an end to the curse on all women of alienation from God and subservience to men. Lest anyone miss the point, Jesus, in the exercise of His ministry, makes woman's restoration very clear. All of this was the result of her response: "Be it done unto me according to Thy Word." With that offering of Self to the fulfillment of the Will of God, Mary was put on a par with God-made-man in the Person of Jesus. And Jesus attested to this ascendancy, "Who does the will of My Father in Heaven is My brother, and sister, and mother."

And so it was that God kept His promise of Redemption; man and woman, once again as *one* being equal in purpose and power; *one* being together; a created expression of the unity in the Godhead. "You are now no longer male or female, but a new Creation." And it was to this new Creation, male and female, that the power to perpetuate throughout time, was given. Not one or the other. Not one over the other; but to both as *ONE*.

The Roman Church is failing to accept the will of God in God's full restoration of women, now baptized into His person and empowered with His mission.

God's redeeming love called Woman to be with Him as a *mediator*. "They have no wine," she said to Jesus speaking of the hosts at the wedding feast at Cana. Her plea prompted Jesus to work His first public miracle.

His redeeming love called Woman to comfort Him as a *friend*. "In the course of their journey, He came to a village; and a woman named Martha welcomed Him to her house."

His redeeming love called woman to be a *disciple*, "Mary sat down at the Lord's feet and listened to Him speaking."

His redeeming love called Woman to *apostleship*, "Now, after this, He made His way through the towns and villages, preaching, proclaiming the Good News of the Kingdom of God. With Him went the twelve, as well as certain women."

His redeeming love called Woman to *share the secret* of Who He is. "And He said to the woman at the well, 'I, who am speaking to you, I am the Christ.'"

His redeeming love confirmed her *priesthood* for all to see as she stood anguished and agonized, broken and poured out as her beloved Son was crucified. "Beneath the Cross of Jesus stood His Mother, and His Mother's sister, Mary, the wife of Cleophas, and Mary of Magdala.

During the crucifixion events, with the exception of John the Evangelist, the men and some of the women had made their escape, Judas had betrayed Jesus for a bag of money, Peter had denied following Jesus, and all the rest fled the crowd and cowered in hiding in an upper room, fearful for their lives and what their having aligned themselves with Jesus, now disgraced, would forebode for their future.

Momentarily frightened and confused, they may have been finished with Jesus; but Jesus was not finished with them. He was going to send them the Holy Spirit. But first, He had to arise. The male apostles were not there for this creation-altering miracle. But the women were there. The women would be the witnesses of this history-altering event. As a result, Jesus ordained them the first preachers of the most significant occurrence in all of human history. "Go," He said to Mary, following her embrace of Him, "find the brothers and tell them that I have risen; and I am ascending to my Father, to My God and to your God." And so, Mary went and declared to them: "I have seen the Lord!"

Paul refers to the Resurrection of Jesus as the one single most important event in all of history. So important is this event that had it not occurred, nothing else would have mattered. "If Christ be not risen," Paul testifies, "our faith is in vain, and we are, in all of creation, the most to be pitied."

And Jesus gave to a woman the privilege of bringing this news to the rest of His chosen community. No wonder Mary could say without the least hesitation:

> "My soul magnifies the Lord
> My spirit finds its joy in God, my Savior...
> For He has looked with pity upon the humiliation
> of His handmaid
> And now, henceforth and forever more,
> All generations shall call me blessed..."

As we look at society today, we see women moving up, taking their place as leaders in all spheres of human endeavor – except for much of the global Christian Church. One has to wonder if women feel blessed in the Ecclesial Community. One has to wonder how long the Roman Church will repudiate the complete liberating grace of the Incarnation and perpetuate the chauvinistic attitudes, behaviors, and structures that were the result of sin.

According to Paul, "All creation is waiting for our revelation as children of God." This unity and this equality, this creation of society according to the Will of God – a society in which all are valued as Temples of the Holy Spirit, where our values and pursuits reflect the teachings of Jesus, *this* is the goal of our ministerial strivings.

No matter what is said, or by whom, or about what –
until and unless our organizations lead the Ecclesial
Community to becoming the fulfillment of the
Incarnation event, the event that Jesus defines as one in
which He has come so that "All may have life and have
it in all its fullness," we will be impediments to the Will
of God.

Jesus' resurrection confirmed the authenticity of His
claim, His mission, and His power. Those who claim to
follow Him are not free to ignore nor change the agenda.

And so, the women and the men who claimed Him as
their Leader, stood by and watched
as He bade them farewell and was miraculously lifted
up to the Heavens, and disappeared from the sight.

Yet, He kept His promise. He did "not leave them
orphans." They retired again to the upper room,
unafraid, fully surrendered to His agenda, determined to
bring Divine Life back to the human experience, "And
the Holy Spirit descended upon *every one of them*," the
men and the women gathered there. And the Ecclesial
Community was born.

As our Church clings to the pre-redemptive
consequence of humanity's fall from grace, it is no
wonder that the ordained priesthood is being
diminished. The exclusion of women is a perpetuation
of the consequences of sin, of the disorder caused by
sin. The Roman Church today has a unique opportunity
to go through the process of discernment about women
as priests. Hopefully, the Church will cling to the

scripture, "The Kingdom of God is within you." If it is truly the "Kingdom of God," it is a unifying experience where all are equal and free to use their gifts and talents as led by the Holy Spirit to achieve God's Will in the world: "Now you are no longer male nor female, but a new Creation...a holy nation, a chosen people, a royal priesthood." Anything less is a rejection, a sinful repudiation of the full redemptive work of Christ.

Again, I returned to the shadows, reflecting on the hard questions, the only truly essential questions: "Why do we walk as if we're still under the power of sin? Why do we still follow the law of sin? Why do we conduct ourselves as if the Savior had never come?"

"Prayer"

The Masai women chant their prayer in quiet confidence. Almighty God, Nursing Mother, remember what suits us. The Christ, the Savior, Jesus, chants His anguished cry from the Cross, "Father, into your hands, I surrender My Spirit."

Father-Mother God, Man-Woman God. Somehow masculine-feminine speaks Yahweh. Not one nor the other alone can image Him. For it was Yahweh who said, "Let us make humans to our image and likeness. Male and female He made them."

Mother-Father God, have mercy on us. Forgive us our clinging to separateness, our competitive spirit. Forgive us our walls of steel and iron and brick and mortar. Forgive us our fences of class and race and gender and dogma. Forgive us our trenches of nationality and ethnicity and culture.

Forgive us our UN-ONENESS.

14   Righteousness

It is written in the Book of Micah, Chapter 6, Verse 8: "This is what Yahweh asks of you, only this: To act justly, to love tenderly, and to walk humbly with your God." To do this is to understand that "God is Truth."

I was thinking of the *Virtue of Doubt*. It has to be more than an intellectual exercise. More than mere posturing. It's more than a concept. It's more than an emotion. It's its own type of conviction. It says: Truth is larger than any one person, movement, idea. It is larger than rite, ritual, sacrament, sacrifice. It shines on all of these like stars on the blackness, shedding a little bit of light in each one. Each human being, each human experience, each natural phenomenon will receive and reflect a little light. The more we can come together, the larger the light becomes. And the brighter it becomes, the more the need for dogma and doctrine diminishes. The road to God becomes simpler and clearer, and less encumbered, even to appreciate the revelation that: "If your conscious does not accuse you, you have not sinned." We may attempt to impose our dogmas, theologies, doctrines, liturgies on others in order to declare them brothers/sisters. But God gave us no freedom to judge. We come to not only accept, but to embrace this position. And it leads to that freedom promised by Jesus: "If the Son sets you free, you are free, indeed."

And so, this is what Yahweh asks of us, only this: To act justly, to love tenderly, and to walk humbly with our

God. To understand this is to understand that God is TRUTH.

When we think of justice, we think of giving to all persons that which is their due. But Justice, in Biblical terms, goes far beyond this. It is a call to righteousness, to respond rightly in all circumstances. It is a call to wholeness and holiness of life. It requires that we develop a mystical view of reality so that we can perceive the whole creation as it is seen by the Creator, in order that we may relate to it according to His pre-determined law. It demands that we respond in complete honesty in every relationship-with God, ourselves, and each other. It demands that we operate within the Truth about all reality as best we can understand it. Scripture describes God as TRUTH.

To love tenderly. There's nothing sentimental in this, nothing passive. The Christian virtue of love, by its very nature, seeks always to function within the framework of the truth and to operate out of that framework. It is sometimes risky, even dangerous. It is most often a very hard reality. Maybe that's why Yahweh calls us to exercise a "tender" love. Tenderness implies a lightness of touch, a reverent caution, a gentle concern that is far more than an intellectual experience. True tenderness has a deeply emotional and empathetic component. It brings to the exercise of love, however difficult, the redeeming element of compassion. It demands that we operate within the Truth about relationships.

To walk humbly. Again, humility is that virtue which situates us solidly in Truth. It calls us to be done with pretention, masks, posturing; to reach for honesty and goodness; to learn what it means to be simple; to know one's gifts and limitations; to live with a grateful heart, in an attitude of waiting for the Lord; to do the things that are pleasing to God. It demands that we operate within the Truth about ourselves, and be thankful for our creation that moves us through cleansing episodes of temporary pain that prepares us for a life of eternal joy.

And so, we can, in all honesty, say, "Thank You God, for Creating Me."

I give You thanks, O Creator mine
That You have made me so,
A wondrous little gift of earth,
Your image – mine to glow.

Oh, I will hold me in my heart
And to myself be true,
For being truly who I am
Is how I honor You.

I shall not spoil Your gift of me
So carefully divined,
For deep within my heart I know
That I am truly Thine.

I know I'm not quite finished now,
In fact, I've hardly just begun,
For I have mountains yet to climb
And miles of road to run.

But I will make my life unfold
As You would have me be
To merge my being into Yours
For all eternity.

O gentle, loving Creator mine,
Please help me grow like You,
For this is how to guard Your trust,
And to us both be true.

"Prodigal Son"

*Now we are no longer to take into
account whether or not a person is
male or female, Easterner or Westerner,
bound or free, Black or White or
Yellow or Red or Brown, for we all
have become One in Christ Jesus;
and in Him, we are a new Creation.*

111

15   No More -Isms

In the second chapter of the *Acts of the Apostles*, Saint Luke gives us a brief account of the "Descent of the Holy Spirit" and the subsequent "Miracle of Tongues." He writes, "All were filled with the Holy Spirit... and they began to express themselves in foreign tongues. Staying in Jerusalem at the time were devout Jews of every nation under heaven. These heard the sound and assembled in a large crowd. They were much astonished because each one heard these men speaking their own language. 'Are not all of these men speaking Galileans?' they asked. 'How is it that each of us hears them in our native language?'"

Again, in Chapter 15 of *Acts*, where Luke gives an account of the Council of Jerusalem, the question dealt with was that of forced circumcision of the Gentile converts in accordance with Mosaic practice. Peter, of course, had already had the vision that helped him understand not to call "unclean what God has cleansed," so he was able to settle the dispute by asking the provocative question: "Why then do you put God to the test by trying to place on the shoulders of these converts a yoke which neither we nor our fathers were able to bear?" He concludes, "Our belief is rather that we were saved by the favor of the Lord, Jesus, and so are they."

It would seem from these events that the Holy Spirit taught the early Christians a different view of "universality" than has been in vogue in the Church since the conversion of Constantine in 325 A.D. Evangelization seems to have shifted from one of

112

bringing the Good News to the people in their own language and customs to that of forcing an acceptance of Christianity in the dress and behavior and value system of White Western civilization, and weaving Gospel and culture so closely together that the mesh of one is seen to be inseparable from that of the other. This, perhaps, more than any other factor, including the personal sins of both the individual Christians and the corporate Church, has dealt a near lethal blow to the credibility of Christian witness.

For to be truly acceptable and accepted in the Christian Church, one becomes a believer not only in Jesus Christ, but also in all those "isms" by which Western civilization defines itself, including nationalism, capitalism, pragmatism, separatism, racism, and male chauvinism.

This cultural imperialism linked to the Christian message results in estrangement for many non-White, non-Western peoples seeking examples of lived Biblical Christianity in order to convert. The last three 'isms" in particular have been very large stumbling blocks to the conversion of North American Blacks to the Roman Catholic Church. Let us look briefly at these three. With no real Light, I began to suck on the darkness.

Separatism, which might metaphorically be described as "each rat in his own hole," runs counter to a well-defined sense of mutuality and one-likeness as experienced by the Black Community. The separatist tendency among North American Whites can be readily understood by anyone familiar with the history of rivalry and intense nationalism among the White peoples of Europe. The European immigrants did not divest themselves of these narrow loyalties when they landed on American soil. Instead, they set up their separate neighborhoods and churches and remained, insofar as they were able, isolated units composed of diverse ethnic groups.

The Black experience in North America was quite different. Though Blacks, brought to this country as slaves, came from different parts of Africa and from difference African tribes, they were not allowed the luxury of maintaining their distinct customs, culture, and language. In fact, everything generic to the African experience as a whole, and specific to whatever particular African tribe, was ruthlessly eradicated. In the horror of this lost identity and in the mutuality of this holocaust of slavery, Black people developed an all-inclusive sense of community. To be Black was to "belong." Blacks from whatever background no longer had any unique stories to tell, for the whole race had become one story - that of painful survival. Educated and uneducated, racially mixed and unmixed, Easterner and Westerner, male and female, slave and freeman sat down together and broke bread in a fellowship of shared oppression.

Here was the *melting pot* indeed, as opposed to the *smorgasbord* of White ethnicity. Such community at the gut level could not be easily satisfied in a Church such as the Catholic Church where Community is more a matter of theological definition than a lived experience.

114

Racism. Blacks received the Christian message of the Fatherhood of God and the brotherhood of man, universal salvation, human equality, and mutual love from a people who not only practiced ethnic separatism, but also fomented a philosophy of superiority within the human family based solely on the degree of pigmentation in the human skin. It is a paradoxical situation that continues to puzzle Blacks to this day. And even after having endured nearly three hundred years of the cruelest slavery in the recorded history of peoples, and of another hundred years of segregation, and of the present trend to change the appearance but not the substance of Jim Crowism, Blacks still believe and still live in hope that somewhere down the line, preachment and practice will finally come together. When this can happen in the Catholic Church, converting Blacks will no longer be difficult. Meanwhile, while racism pervades the climate of the country and the Church as an integral cultural component, for Blacks to find themselves in a Church that is quantitatively and qualitatively controlled and dominated by White Europeans and Americans is too reminiscent of the old relationships between Blacks and Whites in the slave society. After all, there is in the minds of Blacks an appreciable similarity between the "White Father" and the "White Master," at least, on the surface.

Male Chauvinism. The Christian Community, in too many instances, has ignored the Biblical concept of equality in service. One is hard put to find anywhere in Christendom any real examples of "let the greatest among you be the servant of all" or "each according to his/her gift." The Catholic Church, in particular, with its rigid hierarchism and its systematic exclusion of women from Sacramental positions of leadership and authority, would have little appeal to a people that long ago lost its tendency toward structures of chauvinism in the day-to-day struggle for survival; and it was precisely in that survival struggle that the Black woman was forged into a leader and an equal with her male counterpart. In fact, it may even have given the Black female an edge over the male.

The ever-present heart of the White Master's house and the perpetual object of his lust, the Black female became the ears for his whispered plans, the source of forbidden sustenance, both spiritual and material, for her own people, and the mediatrix that constantly mitigated the Master's wrath against them. And though the Black male is, at last, coming into his own, it is not likely that the strength developed in the Black woman through her personal suffering and her peculiar position in the slave society can now be harnessed and held back in order to satisfy any White male ego structure, whether religious or secular, for the entire race, including the male, profits from her continued strength. Therefore, of the many teachings of Saint Paul, the Church that arrives at Paul's final realization that, in the call of Jesus, it is "...neither male or female, but a new creation," is more likely to attract the Black Community than the ones that lag behind in the earlier darkness of that pre-Christian mentality, still under the influence of patriarchalism, that declares, "Let women be silent in the Church."

If, then, Blacks are to have a future in the Catholic Church, the large questions to be answered are: (1) Can the Church return to her original call to universality in which the Gospel, unfettered by cultural ties, can be preached in its pristine purity and incarnated in the language and culture of the people to be evangelized? "Each of us hears in his own native tongue." (2) While retaining this deeper sense of universality, can the Church rise above its tendency to cater to the whims of separatist groups, especially those resulting from ethnic, national, and racial prejudices, and create both a community of witness and witness to community, to unity, so that the world may see realized the prayer of Jesus: "That they all may be one as Thou, Father, in Me, and I in Thee?" (3) Can the Church move, as Jesus did, beyond the sexist demands of the patriarchal mentality brought over from the Jewish Faith to the full recognition of the "Gifts of the Spirit" rather than the gender of the flesh? "Mary, go to My brothers and tell them, 'I am ascending to My Father and to your Father, to My God and to your God.' Mary went to the disciples and announced, 'I have seen the Lord.'" (4) And finally, can the Church democratize its hierarchical structures making possible an equality of brotherhood and sisterhood as envisioned by Jesus?

"The pagans who have authority lord it over one another, but it is not to be so among you.... All you are brothers and sisters. And call no man your father. For you have only one Father, God, who is in heaven." And, "let he(she) who would be first among you become the servant of all."

In short, can the Churches in their structures, leaders, and membership finally reflect the Gospel that they so eloquently preach to others? "The *media* is the *message.*" When the answers to all these questions are positive, then Blacks, and many other peoples as well, will find a home and have a future in the Catholic Church, and other denominations in the Christian Ecclesial Community.

"The Nativity"

And I say to you…
Do not let your prayers
be like those of the Pharisees
who, in their much praying,
think they will be heard.
No, when you pray say simply
OUR FATHER… for the Father
knows all your needs even
before you present them to Him.

16   I Pray

Somehow, I could never quite get the message straight. On the issue of prayer, the light just didn't seem to shine clearly.

The subject of prayer has always been one of deep concern for me. I don't mean the neat packaging or labelling by which we attempt to categorize it. Are we asking God for something? Are we thanking Him? Are we worshipping Him? Does it matter which? I've always had some deep inner sense that prayer was less an activity than a condition, a state of being. How else could the Lord have admonished, "Pray always"? Too often I've been confronted with statements like, "I prayed, but it did no good." On one occasion, a friend said to me, "Maybe God has answered all my prayers; but if He did, He spoke in a foreign language."

When I was a child and I first heard the words of Jesus in the Scriptural passage, "Whatever you ask the Father in My Name, He will give to you," I was profoundly moved. Was Christ really serious? Was this a passage to be taken literally?

Did that "Whatever" cover everything? If it did, would there be any sick and dying? Would there be wars and rumors of wars? Would there be accidents, natural tragedies? Would there be any poor and dispossessed? Etc. I thought over the innumerable things that I had asked for and had not received. Already in my young life I was learning to strike bargains with God. "I'll do this for You, God, if You do that for me." Already in my young life, I was sensing that God had favorites. I couldn't reach Him from my "low on the totem pole" status in the Mystical Body, but there was Anthony to find my lost objects, Christopher to make my travels safe, Blaze to keep my throat well, the Guardian Angel to watch over my every move, Michael to protect me from "Satan's snare," etc., and Jude when all else failed. And, of course, there was the Mother of God, the Mediatrix of all graces, to keep that "created God-life coming always my way. I'd be given a patron Saint at Baptism and Confirmation. I'd learn how to "bank indulgences" and overpower an intractable God with "storm novenas."

Sacrifice was an inevitable part of making prayer work. After all, didn't the Israelites win battles as long as Moses prayed with his arms outstretched? So, you could pray standing, but kneeling was better. You could speak the words, but singing was twice as good. You could say one Hail Mary, but better would be fifty. Etc. And if you counted those fifty on "blessed" beads, they were a virtual powerhouse.

The Mass had its unique efficacy, because in it, it was Jesus who prayed, Jesus who was offered to God at the "Bargaining table." Of course, though one Mass had eternal value (nothing about Christ being limited), still a novena of Masses somehow had an even more "eternal" value.

I don't know at what point I became suspicious of this "business" of prayer, this "busy-ness" about prayer, this "science" of bargaining with God as if He were some merchant in a market stall. The suspicion may not even have grown all at once, but gradually over a period of time. It may have been conceived after reading: "Do not let your prayer be like that of the Pharisees who, because of their much saying, think that they shall be heard." The gestation period may have been nurtured by such salient food as: "We do not know what to ask for when we pray, but the Spirit pleads for us with unutterable groaning."

Yet, our Divine Savior did honor the Apostles' request by telling them, "When you pray say, our Father, Who art in heaven," and went on to teach them what we have come to call "The Lord's Prayer," a prayer that speaks both to God's glory and our fundamental spiritual and temporal needs.

Am I wrong in believing, then, that prayer is more a state of being than an activity? And if it is only an activity, one of praising, thanking, asking, why then does so much seem to achieve so little? And has Jesus deceived us with His promise, "Whatever You ask the Father in My Name will be granted you."?

If we have read those lines and felt betrayed when our prayers did not seem to be answered, is it, perhaps, that we have not really understood them, have not focused on the phrase "in My Name" which qualifies the promise?

The question is often flippantly asked, "What's in a name?" Jesus is a name that describes the promised Savior, Christ, the Anointed One. Perhaps no name has so spoken the meaning, purpose, promise, and mission of the person named so eloquently and so well as that name, Jesus Christ, given to that Man who became:

- The Pascal Offering in the struggle between darkness and light.
- The Light that the darkness could not comprehend.
- The Beloved Son in Whom the Father was well-pleased.
- The Incarnate Word of the all-powerful God who was "meek and humble of heart."
- The Temple that would raise itself in three days.
- The Stone which the builders rejected, who became the cornerstone.
- The great High Priest who did not have to offer sacrifice first for His own sin, for no one could convict Him of sin.
- The Lamb of God who takes away the sins of the world.

All of this is in His name, the name of Jesus, meaning Savior. It was for this mission that the Father had sent Him into the world; and according to His own testimony, He never deviated from it. Jesus attests "I do always the things that are pleasing to Him."

A person who says, "I come in the name of ....." Shouldn't the mission of that person reflect the interests of the one in whose name she/he has come? Therefore, when we approach the Father in Christ's name, it is clear that our petition must concern itself with those interests consistent with the mission and meaning of Christ, or it cannot be said to be "in the name of Christ."

But this kind of prayer, in the name of Jesus, growing out of concern for His mission and meaning, if it is to be authentic, must flow from a heart completely surrendered, completely given; one who, even as Christ, seeks "to do always the things that are pleasing" to the Father; one who, even as Christ, finds that his/her "meat is to do the Father's Will"; one for whom the lovely cry of the Psalmist, "The Lord is my Shepherd/Indeed nothing shall I want," is no longer a mere poetic statement, nor even a pious hope, but rather a genuine condition of being. This one can pray and will be heard, for this one comes not to seek his/her own will, but the will of Jesus in whose name he/she has come.

Am I deep in the shadows? It seems that the sad thing that has happened relative to prayer is that we have turned its whole purpose topsy-turvy. Prayer, defined simply by the theologians as "the lifting up of the heart and mind to God," seems to be right. It is not the bringing down of God's heart and mind to us. In the initial stages, prayer is meant to assist us in knowing, loving, embracing and doing the will of the Father; and as it matures in us, lead to a loving union with Him already in this life in preparation for the final union when we shall see Him "face to face." Is not, then, the "Ask and you shall receive, seek and you shall find, knock and it shall be opened to you," concerned precisely with this relationship?

It seemed unfortunate to me that this is seldom our purpose in prayer. Instead of praying to make ourselves conformable to God's will, we generally pray in an attempt to make God conformable to our will. Even worse, our prayer would reduce Him to the level of a steward, a servant, or even a slave at our disposal, His almighty power bent to fulfill our every capricious desire. This habitual abuse of prayer can only maintain us in a state of spiritual infancy akin to actual physical infancy in which our own temporal and tangible gratification is the only perceivable good.

But once we accept the testimony of Christ that; "One is Good, God alone," then it becomes quite obvious that prayer can be efficacious only when it is in pursuit of that very same Good. Only that kind of prayer can be said in the name of Jesus; and when it is, it will be answered, for God cannot work against Himself. The other type of prayer actually evidences a lack of faith, and Jesus has already testified that "He could work no miracles in that town because of (their) unbelief."

"The Pieta"

And...
Jesus bent down and started writing on the ground with HIS finger. When they persisted in their questioning, He straightened up and said to them, "Let the man among you who has no sin be the first to cast a stone at her." A second time, He bent down and wrote on the ground. Then the accusers drifted away one by one, beginning with the elders.

17   Who I Am

Leaving the sunlight and shadows, I reached out to an old friend. We exchanged pleasantries, and then I followed him up a long flight of stairs to the attic. The door squeaked open to a room of exquisite art. "It was all done when I was there," he said. I stood transfixed before a life-size painting of St. Francis, bathing the feet of a leper. "I tried to break the habit," he went on, "but I couldn't. It was the only way I could pray. It's the cleanest worship I'm capable of." He put his hand on my shoulder. "You're lucky," he said. "You're in a community of women who appreciates the arts."

That was true. And perhaps, it was true, more or less, of all communities of women, especially with regards to music and the plastic arts. My research had indicated that the writer was the one artist who, apparently, had little formal recognition in any religious community prior to '63.

"Well, Brother," I said (I had not gotten over the habit of calling him Brother), "someday that will change. I do know a few women artists in Religious Community. Of course, their art is not their primary apostolate. It's something they do after a full day's work at something else."

When we went downstairs and I had gone out once more to walk alone beneath the stars on that quiet summer evening, I kept reflecting on the plight of Brother Jacob. I had known other artists who, for whatever reasons, could not make it in Religious Communities. Was there

127

in Convents and Monasteries some kind of conspiracy against the Artist? Religious were certainly appreciative of art. Why not, then, of artists? Was it, perhaps, that no theologian had given the artist a prominent place in any listing of apostolic imperatives? Or had they? And if they hadn't, why not? Why had they categorized the Savior only as Priest, Prophet, and King? Was He not minstrel as well, an itinerant preacher, a wandering storyteller? It seemed to me that the arts are an integral part of the apostolate of the Church. For while historians record the events that shaped the past and prophets pinpoint the values and trends that will shape the future, artists hold up a mirror to the present in which both the past is reflected and the future is foretold. They do this while delighting, entertaining, intriguing, informing, shaping, and, in general, calling us unsuspectingly to stretch beyond our normal reach. Such is the power of the artist. Rarely is truth ever more delightful, more cathartic, more readily accepted, as when it is presented in the form of art.

The question should be dealt with: Can art ever be thought of as an authentic Christian ministry, and the artist as minister? Recently, I had the opportunity to spend some time with Religious men and women who were grappling with that question. Most responded to it with a facile *yes*. But continued discussion and further examination revealed that few are encouraged in their respective communities to pursue artistic expression on a serious and full-time basis as an authentic ministry. The end result of that state of affairs seems to have prompted a slow attrition of real artists from Religious Communities.

Too often the artists among us are expected to repress their peculiar genius in favor of more "practical" forms of ministry; or, at most, find time for their art between, before, or after other full-time duties. And, of all the artists in our midst, writers seem to be the least appreciated and the least understood. Because musicians, painters, sculptors, and related artists have made some headway toward recognition in some communities, I focus my remarks on the *writer as minister*, for I believe that the writer, whether this be in the genre of fiction, non-fiction, or poetry, has generally faced a harder battle for recognition.

Jesus, Eternal NOW

May we submerge our separate histories
In His story?
And lose our dreams of grandeur
In His glory?
As we learn that - though we may be broken-hearted –
It was not He who from our life departed.

Our every Fiat generates His Incarnation,
The ever-present and eternal NOW;
He is cocooned in every YES we speak
And every call to which we humbly bow;
He's not some distant Vision to await,
And thus, our lives entwined with His, we celebrate.

Of All Things for Which I Long

Of all things for which I long
    I long to change them all;
And place my new design before the gods
    in their assembly hall;
That nothing more from nature come
    and nothing more from art;
No gift however great or small
    that did not please the heart.

It is important at the very outset to distinguish the artist-writer from the person who simply writes, because it bears directly on some of the problems that artists have encountered in Religious Community. The answer, I think, deals with the question not only of the peculiar genius we attribute to the artists but, perhaps, more specifically, with the intrinsic motivation out of which their art proceeds.

Persons who simply write are moved by a very different dynamic from that of the artist-writer. Persons who simply write use writing as a tool in the service of some other kind of endeavor. They use it as a means to an end that is completely apart from the writing itself. For example, they might write to make money; then their writing would be in the service of economics. They might write to get a message out. Writing, then, is in the service of communication. The telephone could be just as useful and would probably be more effective. They might just want to see their name in print. Hence, their writing would be in the service of vanity.

The point is, that persons who simply write are not motivated, not enlivened, not driven by the *need* to write. The majority of writers belong to this class.

Artist-writers, on the other hand, are those who cannot *not* write. A telephone could never be the means by which they communicate their messages. Descartes said, "I think, therefore I am." Artist-Writers say, "I write, therefore I am." Writing is the very fuel that sparks their energy. It defines their purpose. It gives validity to their existence. It is perceived by them as the most authentic and fundamental expression of who they are. It is radically self-creative for them, and its product is its own end. This, I believe, is at the very core of the problem artists experience in Religious Institutes. Most real artists do not survive in them, because Religious Communities, over the centuries, have come to identify themselves as existing for something other than the actualization of the unique potential of their individual members. This shift in emphasis has been sanctified, legitimized by what has come to be called the "apostolic model." Too many communities today are extrinsically oriented. They are placed at the service of others. They are no longer dynamically and fundamentally involved with the most sacred of all action—the *creation of the self.* Some find it too hard to really hear the message that the "minister is the ministry." But Christ attests to that wisdom: "That they may be sanctified," He declared, "I sanctify myself."

The pragmatic and utilitarian orientations of Western society have dulled religious sensitivity to the most radical of all evangelical concepts: that of *becoming.* An apostolate today is almost exclusively identified as *something we do*. It no longer has any relationship, for many of us, *to who we are*. Ministry is tied to *what* we become rather than *who* we become—or *who* we serve rather than *who we are* that serve.

The first revelation about God is that He is Creator. And the first revelation about human life (man-woman) is that we are made in the image of God. This being so, the act of creating, is not just something some of us do. It flows from the very essence of who we are in the deepest core of our being as images of the God who made us.

The true artist, then, is driven from that center, that same center from which ministry authenticates itself, because it is in that center that worship really begins. It gives worship its real name—the ability to say *Yes* to God in response to the discovery of *who one is*. There is essentially no other worship and no other religious life than that. This *Yes* is the fullness of poverty, chastity, and obedience. Once we understand this, we come to know that ministry can never be anything more profound nor more mysterious than that of creating a climate which facilitates the efforts of others to discover who they are and to utter their own unique *yes*.

In this endeavor, artists have a special role because the work of art, both in its creation and appreciation, prepares the human psyche for that contemplation which is necessary to self-knowledge; a self-knowledge which is, in its turn, necessary for a fuller knowledge of reality. Without self-knowledge and a continually growing knowledge of reality, it is difficult to achieve that fullness of worship that our *yes* implies; and it is equally difficult to be an effective minister. Both types of knowledge are necessary for worship and for ministry because they are a response to the movement of the Spirit, to a grace-filled call from God acting in all of creation. However, the Lord does not call except by *name*.

Artists open themselves and others to call forth the contemplation required for the creation or appreciation of their art—thus making a unique contribution in preparation of the human psyche for worship and ministry. Artists, in fact, may be indispensable to worship and ministry because contemplation is indispensable.

What I have said is true of all art. It is true, therefore, also of artist-writers who participate in this unique call. They make a statement that lasts, that situates itself within the function of ministry, that has this quality of ministering by dealing with the expression of the universal within the particular. This task requires that they be constantly alert to that which is unique, and to every detail of that which is unique, while never losing sight of its substantial unity with the whole of reality.

Artist-Writer Ministers are in the perpetual grip of paradox. Profoundly alone, they are deeply involved with the crowd. Profoundly introverted, their art gives rise in them for a need to reach out. Acutely aware of the transitory nature of all things, they unceasingly probe for that which is immutable.

I believe that writers are artists who have the burden of achieving through written symbols even more than the painter does with brush and pigment, for they bring with the use of these symbols, not only texture and color, but also odor and sound, and every other sensation capable of stimulating the inner senses of the mind. Artist-Writers are musicians, sensitively attuned to the music of their instrument which is the word, and to the rhythm and beat of phrase and sentence. They are historians who must have a profound sense of time while never losing touch with the reality of timelessness. Artist-writers are children of the moment while, at the same time, transcending it. They must develop the capacity to reflect on the experience of the senses, to probe the root causes of human experience, and to reveal these in unique literary expressions without judgement, and to foreshadow their outcome without prophesying.

The Artist-Writer Ministers, unlike preachers and prophets, are not *should* and *ought* persons. They do not attempt to teach with proverbs, nor to heal with platitudes, but to allow the imaged word to reflect a personal, relational, and/or societal reality. Their imaginative flights open the psyche to ever new and greater possibilities, for they point toward what could be with the same precision with which they record what has been or what is.

Artist-Writer Ministers are, finally, imitators of the Father. The ultimate perfection of their ministry is, as was the Father's, *to make their work become flesh.*

The Latins call it: "La mistica de la noche," the mystique of the night. Maybe it was that and nothing more, for, indeed, the night was "far spent." And yet I went on sitting in the abandoned "upper room" where earlier in the evening we had gathered for prayers. It was one of those strange paradoxes that "prayer" most often happened in me after "prayers" were over and the community had gone—each to her own way. I sat alone and my heart was overflowing with the sweetness of the Lord as I contemplated the scenes in the attic room. Brother Jacob's art had laid the Lord in my bosom and I could not leave off nurturing Him there. I stood, trembling, with Brother Jacob's portrait of the adulterous woman, and mentally I bent over to read the Savior's scrawl that would set her free. Then I got to my knees and reflected on the account in John's Gospel once again.

The Scribes and the Pharisees led a woman forward who had been caught in adultery. They made her stand there in front of everyone. "Teacher." they said to Him, "this woman has been caught in the act of adultery. In the law, Moses ordered that such women should be stoned.

What do you have to say about the case? "Jesus bent down and started writing on the ground with His finger. When they persisted in their questioning, he straightened up and said to them, "Let the man among you who has no sin in him be the first to cast a stone at her." A second time, He bent down and wrote on the ground, Then the audience drifted away, one by one, beginning with the elders.

18   Calling

One cannot help but marvel at the awesome power of the written word of an Artist-Minister. In spite of this reality, Artist-Writers might very well find themselves in conflict within their Religious Community. That shift, discussed earlier, from an emphasis upon *becoming* what God has made of each of us to that of communicating what God has done by means extrinsic to our person—tends to alienate the Artist. This tendency of Religious to find their glory, their sense of worth, not in *being* but in *doing*, and to express their reason for being as primarily responding to a perceived need in others, is opposed to that of Artists who function out of a perceived need within themselves. Artists understand, as few others can, the anguish expressed by John Milton in that famous sonnet, "On His Blindness."

> When I consider how my light is spent
> E'er half my days in this dark world and wide
> And that one talent which was death to hide
> Lodged with me useless, though my soul more bent
> To serve therewith my Maker and present
> My true account, lest He returning, chide....

I believe that it is one of the present-day challenges facing Ecclesial Communities to reinstate Artists, precisely as artists, and to develop that theology that will free them to function without guilt, and to receive and promote their work as an integral offering in the total ministerial role of the Churches. For there are few who are as gifted as Artists who can see reality and who are empowered to make it visible, that is seeable by others—with such forcefulness, immediacy, poignancy, and even pleasure. To quote Sister Christa Mirani of The Detroit Province of the Sisters of Mercy, "The Artist lives at the point of pain; and the Artist as writer keeps the world uncomfortable because this pain forces her/him to keep the elegant questions, the truly significant questions, alive."

If not theology, history evidences the significance of art and the power of the written word. Every conquering army that hoped to consolidate its new power took measures to control the arts.

In dictatorships and totalitarian states, one of the first freedoms to go is the freedom of the press. In our society, sociologists no longer question the efficacy of the media, both written and electronic, as an agent for change, as a power in shaping social values for better or for worse, as the prime educator of both old and young, and as the chief means of raising consciousness from one of narrow provincial concerns to that which embraces the whole of humanity in global perspective. Ecclesial Communities have no better means available to them now for extending the fruits of their communal and personal contemplation and sanctity beyond themselves, and of fulfilling Christ's mandate to "Go into the whole world and teach what I have commanded you" than that of developing the ministerial power of their Artists, and enabling them as well to make maximum use of the media.

By way of graphic illustration, a Religious working in a Catholic elementary school over a period of fifty years will meet (and hopefully influence for good) an average of about twenty-five hundred pupils—allowing that each year she will have about fifty pupils in her classroom. One book, usually written within a year, even if only partially successful, has the potential for reaching (and hopefully influencing for good) an estimated twenty-five thousand persons. If it is greatly successful, it may reach the million or more mark. Imagine the influence of a successful writer over a mere ten-year period.

This is not to diminish the usefulness of formal education in public and private schools; it is simply to draw attention to the power of the media when it is effectively used by ministers of the Word. Artist-Writer Ministers like Chardin, Merton, Kung, Reuther, Greene, Bernanos, and Martin Luther King, Jr., etc. come to mind. Perhaps the greatest credit for the final emancipation of the slaves in this country should go to Harriet Beecher Stowe instead of Abraham Lincoln, for it was she who forced the American society to look at the inhumanity of the situation. Karl Marx gave the first lethal blow to cutthroat capitalism. And on the negative side, Germany gave Adolph Hitler to the world on the strength and popularity of *Mein Kompf.*

Despite the undisputed influence of the media for good or evil, many Religious Communities have clung to their traditional ways of ministering. This is not to say that we do not acknowledge that we have Artists, but we put them to work in other types of service. For example, we see our musicians as useful *teachers* of music; our painters and sculptors as useful *teachers* of art; and our writers as useful *teachers* of grammar and composition. We are not quite sure that artists who simply draw or paint, or musicians who simply play and/or compose music, or writers who simply write quite justify their existence or demonstrate any real usefulness by these activities alone. There is some part of us that still regards the arts suspiciously as something to be done by "rare" and "gifted" individuals in their leisure time. We do not quite buy the argument found in *The Little Prince*, for example, that "because a thing is beautiful, it is truly useful." We have not allowed the creation of art to move from the status of a part-time hobby to that of full-time serious work.

Religious Communities must begin to take advantage of the media in those countries where the free dissemination of ideas has been preserved. And this will not be an easy step to take, for prejudice against the Artist ministering precisely by artistic creation runs deep in Religious Communities. Not too long ago, when I was discussing this problem with a group of Sisters, one dismissed my whole argument with an important shrug. "I'm not against writers," she said. "I like to read. I'm not against any type of artist; but you have to admit, if we start supporting everyone who pretended to be an artist, we'd run the risk of attracting a lot of strange characters to our communities. Artists are such queer types. They can even be freakish. They don't conform, and you never really get to know them. At best, for the Community as a whole, they're useless. And at worst, they're dangerous. They remain strangers in our midst."

I might have said, "By their fruits, you shall know them," but I did not. It would have been too facile. Rather, I left the discussion with the words of the Artist-Writer and lecturer, the Russian-born author, Vladimir Nabokov, racing through my mind.

And I move out of the shadows of internal reflecting, leaving you with those same words: "Stranger," he said, "always rhymes with danger. The meek prophet, the enchanted in his cave, the indignant artist, the non-conforming little school boy—all share in the same sacred danger. And this being so, let us bless them. Let us bless the freak; for in the natural evolution of things, the ape would, perhaps, never have become man (human), had not a freak appeared in the family."

*"And I – when I am lifted up from the earth – will
draw all things to Myself"*

"We Will Not Take Our Pain Too Personally"

*We will not take our pain too personally
But wed it as we must
To the lingering pain of God
Continuously renewed
In every atom of our fallen flesh.*

*We know Him as the Crucified
We feel the Spirit's nurturing hush
That quiets our grieving, aching,
Anxious lives.*

*And throw ourselves into Christ's opened side
To huddle there
Beyond the encroaching grasp of our despair
Waiting for His gentle call to us
To Rise.*

19 Transformation

Real pain, real suffering helps us refocus, helps us to get a different perspective on life. It creates a sense, not only of our powerlessness, but an opening up in us for the action of God's power. One of those paradoxes that you discover is in the shadows of unknowing. What did the soldier say, "There are no atheists in foxholes?" Never are we more aware of our need for God than when we are less able to help ourselves.

"Man's failure is God's opportunity," my father always reminded me whenever I judged myself to have come up short. We get a sense of the God-life, the good-life growing in us, and an ever-growing awareness of the divine pleasure of Yahweh and His involvement with us and His universe. It becomes increasingly clear that Christ is, indeed, the *Door* "through which the sheep must enter." And this is not only an involvement with his Person, historically perceived outside of and apart from us as a solitary Vehicle of our salvation, but also Christ seen as a Sign of what we must become in our own personal lives.

If, in fact, the Wisdom of His Being does not re-shape our lives, we are lost people. By lost, I do not speak of that final "whatever" popularly known as "hell." I mean lost in our day-to-day living, in our moment-by-moment acting and reacting, in our every involvement with ourselves and each other.

Christianity is not so much an institution as a Life. The Christ Being is at once divine and human, supernatural and natural, transcendent and immanent. We must become the same. We must allow His Spirit to reshape and reform the substance of our Being until we reflect exactly that modality. If we fall short in this mystical work, we shall, indeed truly *fall short*.

"He came down
like rain
upon
the fleece,
like showers
watering
the earth."

20 Solidarity

Christmas is the feast of emptying, of opening up our hands and letting go, of finding our oneness with the whole of creation. If Incarnation means anything at all for our troubled lives, it means human solidarity and Communion.

Every year, we Christians take time out from our otherwise, more pragmatic pursuits to celebrate the birth of One whom we call "God in human flesh." Our liturgies are rich with the remembrance. We exchange gifts, for He was Gift. We make good cheer because He said, "Rejoice." We take a holiday; and we let our material abundance overflow to grace and momentarily alleviate the pain of some whom we perceive to be more wretched than ourselves. It is a symbol that we have, at least, a hint of what Christmas really means.

And yet, we have to wonder if it is truly Christmas, truly the birth of God-Made-Man that we have celebrated in all these over two thousand years of Christian history. Have these celebrations helped us rest our egotistical ambitions in the manger of His poverty or find our kinship with such company as ox and ass?

Do we *really know* what Christmas means? For if we did, would we still be clinging with such perverse tenacity to our prejudices and fears? Would we still be trampling one another under foot while we struggle with singular concentration toward the realization of our personal and private aspirations? Would we go on being the fulfillment of the poet's complaint: "wasting our powers" in this business of "getting and spending?"

If we Christians really knew what Christmas meant, would the longed-for promise still be so far away: great nations giving up their thirst for war, hammering their "swords into plowshares and their spears into pruning hooks?" Would not the walls of sexism, racism, elitism, dogmatism, nationalism, and ethnicity, by now, have all come tumbling down? Would the homeless still be languishing in our streets and the hungry searching for sustenance in our garbage cans?

If we Christians really knew what Christmas meant, would we be, like the ancient Philistines, "still clinging to our idols and worshiping the objects that our hands have made?" Would all the signs that speak our Christmas hope, at the first hint of struggle, come so quickly crashing down? Would the lyrics and the melodies be so abruptly stopped? And our prophetic symbols be so unemotionally returned to the dark corners of our closets or the dusty, splintering boards of our attic floors? If we really believed in all that Christmas means, and our hearts even remotely glimpsed the message of the "Word Made Flesh," this alteration in the very life of God, could our lives be left so perennially unaltered?

Again and again, we hear the message of that mysterious night when "Shepherds watched their flocks" and angels sang of "peace on earth." We know

147

the Infant wrapped in swaddling clothes was sent to be the Way. We've heard the call to cultivate His mind, been taught how He left it all to cast His lot with us, become one with our common flesh. ***Incarnation.*** But if He left it all, was it not that He might give it all? "He came down," the psalmist lets us know, "like rain upon the fleece." That's the point we seem not quite to get. *Christmas is the feast of emptying, of opening up our hands and letting go, of finding our oneness with the whole of creation. If Incarnation means anything at all for our troubled lives, it means human solidarity and Communion.*

Perhaps we miss the point because we try to make our spiritual journey much too vertical. Not unlike the builders on the plain of Shinar, we want to construct a tower that allows us to climb directly to the heavens. This is, perhaps, one of our greatest vanities, and it always degenerates into a kind of spiritual Babel. In the Incarnation of Jesus, God reaches down to save us from this temptation. *Christmas is a horizontal feast.* It brings our spiritual journeying back to earth. It reminds us that we are *flesh;* and as Yahweh so eloquently instructs us through the mouth of Job, it is *in flesh that we shall see our God.* It reminds us of the sacred call of human life: to make the earth a mirror of that which is divine.

And so He came to cleanse us of our vanities; to pull our towers down; to set us free from all our false illusions; to take away our idols (all the better worshiped as we hide their visages behind some pseudo-holy masks); and, finally, to give real meaning

148

to our sacrifice and prayer, which is to dispel the darkness from our hearts that obscures our call to sacred productivity for the common good. "As long as you did it to one of these, the least..."

Of course, we Christians long to see the face of God; but how quickly we forget that God in Christ has chosen to be a human face. We Christians long to escape the mundane cares that hold us bound like any other creature not of faith; but how quickly we forget that God in Christ situates Himself in the very midst of all our troubled history. We Christians make our quest for purity in hopes to be transformed by the unique and exquisite joy of some mystical exchange between ourselves and God in some solitary corner far removed. How quickly we forget that God in Christ left just such ecstasy behind that He might sink into our pain, might bear the burden of our fallen flesh, and in this cloak of human woe, walk the earth as one of us who came to serve. We seek, as He did, to be seized by the Spirit of the Lord, forgetting all the while that when we are, "the blind will see, the lame will walk, and the poor will find, in the constancy of our loving friendship with them, the good news that there are no favorites with God."

Whatever our illusions of grandeur may have been, may be, or may become, Christmas will never let us forget that our individual histories are intrinsically interwoven. It gives the total lie to any pretended eloquence by which we seek to extricate ourselves from this unwashed, common mix. Christmas says, there is no longer Jew nor Gentile, slave nor free person; no red, brown, yellow, black nor white; no male nor female; no Roman nor any who are Greek, for all are one in Him. We sing it in the worship that that is our public liturgy and say it in the breaking and sharing of the Sacred Bread:

One Bread, one Body, one Lord of all
One Cup of Blessing which we bless.
And we, though many, throughout the earth,
We are one Body in this one Lord.
Gentile or Jew, servant or free
Woman or man – no more…

"One Body"

If we do not live what we have celebrated in liturgy and song, how can they, who hear us sing, believe? It is not enough to try and stake our claim to holiness by simply greeting an other-than-our-likeness on the way, or momentarily soothing the pangs of a hurting child not perceived to be our own, or by sitting "just a spell" with some lonely and forsaken soul, and then return unmoved, unreconciled, in comfort to our solitary space and hope to find the face of God. Christmas calls us to much more than that. If our dogmas are ever to be more than empty expressions of intellectual arrogance, if our doctrines are ever to be more than faint sketches of momentary illusions, if our liturgies are ever to be more than a vain posturing that impedes rather than assists our worship, we must come to know the divine, come to see *God's face and ours* in that likeness-not-our-own, in that child to whom we gave no birth, in that withered humanity that time and fortune set aside. The solitary cell where we will find true worship is in *the self poured out* for the restoration, the ongoing creation of the other. "I have come," He said, "that they (not I, but *they*) may have life, and have it to the full." That's the kind of feast that Christmas is.

Yes Christmas!
What does it mean?
There are no words
For this mysterious scene:

Shepherds watching, Angels singing
Mighty kings,
Far "away from the madding crowd,"
Paying homage to a little child ~~~
This Hebrew Gift to the Gentile world!

There are no words.
There is no language.
There is no gift of tongues.

The mystery dawns in us
At depths beyond the probe of sensory touch,
Holding us cocooned in speechless wonder
Until, in a kaleidoscope of undulating joy,
The Light breaks through to consciousness
So slow to comprehend.
There are no words to say what means
This "Word-Made-Flesh."

There are no words, and yet
In some slow, unravelling Advent
Of Divine gratuity, we come to know.
And when we know, then there
All our idle dreams, our faulty values,
All the "pomp and circumstance"
Of our wretched, puffed-up lives
Vaporize to nothingness like hissing steam
That fizzles in the open air.

Who would be great when he became so small?
Who would be powerful when He became so weak?
Who would be rich
When He became so poor?
Who would be king
When He aspired to servitude?
Who would seek honor
In the wake of His obscurity?

There are no words, and yet
The message reaches even those who walk away,
Who try to hush its whisper in a cacophony
Of "jingle bells" and "deck the halls,"
In the mash of flesh in shopping malls,

In the shining clutter of snippets
From the wrapping foil,
In the warm cheer
Sloshing in the tinkled glass,
And the kiss of lips
Beneath the mistletoe.

There are no words
That we can say are MINE;
And, yet, we come to know
The human and the Divine
Now intertwined.

"We do not lose heart because our inner being is renewed each day even though our body is being destroyed at the same time. The present burden of our trial is light enough and earns for us an eternal weight of glory beyond all comparison. We do not fix our gaze on what is seen but on what is unseen. What is seen is transitory; what is unseen lasts forever."

21   There Is Light

This *Doubt* that I call *Virtue* is an enlightened doubt. Its vitality, its energy flows from what it knows rather than what it doesn't know. And what it knows *is that it doesn't know*. It has taken into account the fallibility of the entire human condition. It needs no guarantee that by some miracle in the service of faith, the Divine power will alter this human condition. It does not need this miracle because it knows that God does not need it. It knows that Yahweh's Will triumphs no less in human error than in Divine Truth. It attests to the reality that the "light of man is the darkness of God." It has experienced a fleeting shaft of uncreated light that plunges all previous human illuminations into utter blackness. It has come to know an undefinable *reality* in *an unidentified area of being* far away from the probe of sensory power.

The efficacy of this kind of doubt lies in its tendency to make no demands, only inquiry; to be restless with partial answers while knowing that complete answers are never really possible; to avoid webs and to wander in open spaces; to embrace darkness as the womb of light; to delight in the strength of the question while reverencing the fragility of the response; to recognize the detour as a real part of the journey; to know that for those who seek in sincerity, life holds no failures, only experiences.

Finally, then, this *Doubt* that I call *Virtue* is an *enlightened* doubt. Its vitality, its energy flows from what it knows rather than what it doesn't know. And what it knows is that the object of its deepest longing, the one worthy pursuit in all of life is for that Life which is, by human effort, unknowable and unattainable. And so, it rests in the shadows, becomes comfortable with them, not for their own sake, but because it knows that shadows are cast only where there is *Light*.

Author Biographies

SANDRA O. SMITHSON was raised in Nashville, Tennessee, and attended Catholic schools where she excelled in academics, sports, and peer leadership. After graduating with honors from Xavier University, New Orleans, she was granted a teaching fellowship at Fisk University to work toward a Master's in literature. She was recruited to be the first woman to host a talk show on Nashville's first Black radio station, WSOK. Called "A Woman Speaks," her show featured local, national, and world issues in politics, religion, and general social commentary. Due to listener interest, it grew from a 15-minute fill-in spot to a one-hour feature that won first place in the Hooper ratings.

In 1954, she answered an internal call to religious life and joined the School Sisters of St. Francis based in Milwaukee, Wisconsin.

In June 2020, she celebrated 66 years in religious life working in missions in the United States and Central and South America. In Costa Rica in the early 1960s, as principal of a private school, she initiated a pilot educational project for poor children in the surrounding barrio that led to public school reform for the entire country. That era has been referred to as "the Golden Age of Sister Maria Crucis," her religious name at the time. In the mid-1960s, she reclaimed her birth name and now is called "Sister Sandra." She has been an administrator, mentor, teacher, lecturer, writer, negotiator, spiritual leader, and visionary.

In 1992, Sister Sandra founded Project Reflect, a nonprofit organization in Nashville whose mission is "transforming communities through education and policy reform." Sister Sandra was its Executive Director from 1992 through 2014. The organization focused on reading literacy, and in 2000 translated its Reading Success program, written by Mary Smithson Craighead, into computer software, *Reading Success in the Itty Bitty City*. In 2002, Sister Sandra strongly influenced the passage of the first charter school legislation for the State of Tennessee.

Under the new law, in August 2003 Project Reflect opened Middle Tennessee's first free, public charter school, Smithson Craighead Academy (SCA) elementary school, which serves a maximum of 270 children from low-income families. The current population is 50% African-American and 50% Hispanic/Latino.

Sister Sandra continues to work toward excellence in public education for grades K-12 in Tennessee, currently focusing on literacy in grades K-4. She supports parents' right to determine the schools that their children attend with public funds. In turn, the state has the right to require that those schools meet standards of excellence to produce graduates adequately prepared for college, careers, and life.

Sister Sandra's educational philosophy is "inform, reform, and transform." Faith in a God of love undergirds all her work. She volunteers for Project Reflect and Smithson Craighead Academy, and is, at age 94, a corporate (governing) Member of the organization.

She is currently missioned in Nashville, Tennessee, and can be reached, by phone only, at 615-356-5961.

 JACQUELYN SMITHSON HOWARD is a freelance writer and poet originally from Nashville, Tennessee. She writes about our shared experiences of life, love, and triumph; and has used her stories to uplift others. Her father's stroke in 2004 led to a journey of better health, which included her surviving two strokes in 2017 with no mental or physical limitations. Now, her life is sweeter, she has a clarity of vision, and her heart is open to explore the true value of life, unconditional love!

Now, in her sixth decade of writing, Jacquelyn has 14 books to her credit as a poet, writer, storyteller, ghostwriter, contributing author, and public speaker. She is an award-winning published author, and her poetry books are in the private collections of the California State Library and the Special Collections of the Sacramento Public Library.

Once again, Jacquelyn finds strength and clarity in the magical relationship with her father's elder sister. Together, they bridge the generational gap only to discover that they are more alike than either of them could have ever imagined. This book is an opportunity to travel back to the basics. The Teacher and the Student have joined forces to question the logic of what matters most on a variety of topics in this unusual year of civil, political, and climate unrest, as we put the cap on this decade.

Jacquelyn currently resides in Elk Grove, California, and can be reached at itsmytimetosoar@gmail.com.

Made in the USA
Monee, IL
25 August 2021

76478331R00089